A WIDER WORLD

A WIDER WORLD

Portraits in an Adolescence

KATE SIMON

1817

HARPER & ROW, PUBLISHERS · NEW YORK
CAMBRIDGE, PHILADELPHIA, SAN FRANCISCO,
LONDON, MEXICO CITY, SÃO PAULO, SINGAPORE, SYDNEY

For Miriam and Jeremy

FIRST EDITION

Designer: Helene Berinsky

Library of Congress Cataloging-in-Publication Data

Simon, Kate.
   A wider world.

   1. Simon, Kate.   2. Jews—New York (N.Y.)—
Biography.   3. Bronx (New York, N.Y.)—Biography.
4. Adolescent girls—New York (N.Y.)—Biography.
I. Title.
F128.9.J5S59   1986   974.7′27504′0924   [B]   85-45233
ISBN 0-06-015526-4

86 87 88 89 90 RRD 10 9 8 7 6 5 4 3 2

CONTENTS

This is a true story. However, with the exception of members of my family and public figures, the names I have used are not real names.

PRELUDE

The child is a four-year-old immigrant, a vessel of apprehension and hope, sped along the Ellis Island bundles and beards and shawls by her mother, who is carrying in her arms the little brother. The boy must be carried because he is crippled by rickets. There, at the gate to America, stands the tall, handsome father whose mouth, the girl says, is sweet after he kisses her and hands her a piece of the chocolate he is eating. He is God: not the bearded angry old Punisher but the welcomer to dolls whose eyes open and close, the giver of fresh milk, of the fabled, beautiful oranges and the big white eggs which would make her brother strong. The mother had promised all this "when we get to Papa in America," and the little girl's every nerve and vein wants to believe it though she is old in disappointment, old in the fruitless search for the father who had left and stayed away too long. She is old with the burden of taking care of a crippled two-year-old in strange places and strange languages while the mother searches for food, for shelter, for transportation on the month-long journey from Warsaw to Rotterdam and the ship *Susquehanna*.

The family makes the common Jewish immigrant hegira: a few weeks with relatives whose looks and speech are incomprehensible, whose need to love and be loved is a smothering that the little dry stick of a girl slides away from; the little boy, sophisticated in the games of becks and wiles, wallows in it. The next move in the classic journey is to an apartment on Second Avenue and then to East Harlem, where the boy, who is beginning to walk well, and the girl spend as much time as they can steal watching black children who bang drums and wave bright banners as they march in jaunty dance steps, singing in full-throated voices. This is the happy Golden Land as the dour exigencies of the new father is not.

Then we came to Lafontaine Avenue in the Bronx, which gave us Crotona Park for fresh air and trees, newly built schools, and a railroad flat with an indoor toilet all our own, on the top floor of a decently kept tenement. Here we lived from the time I entered elementary school to my first semester in high school. From this house I learned the way to P.S. 58, holding tightly the hand of my brother, a pleasure to tease and to rule and, when the inspiration for quarrels flagged, to play with. It was from this house that I skated on Saturday mornings to the library, an Olympus of kindly goddesses in whose care were hundreds and hundreds of books, all promises of pleasure. It was down these four flights of stairs that I dashed, the inescapable brother in hand, on our way to the movie house at Belmont Avenue and Tremont, to rise and float in luminous clouds along with my sisters in glamour and adventure, Gloria Swanson, Barbara La Marr, Marion Davies. It was on the roof adjacent to this house that I saw for the first time sexual coupling—twisting, bumping, grunting—a stupid, grotesque exercise for a hot summer's afternoon. This couple was as odd as most adults, and although I thought them funnier than the chimpanzees in the Bronx Zoo, I knew that I had had a glimpse of the dark place that belonged to grown-ups only, closed to the innocent eyes of children, or so *they* thought. To maintain the convention I told no one about the roof scene.

Registered in school, the owner of a library card, a steady habitué of the Belmont movies, the penny-a-day customer of a candy store that knew my name, owner of a tree that rained white blossoms in the spring especially for me, and, for a long time, hearing no discussions in the kitchen about moving again, I consented to become a citizen of Lafontaine. Soon the secret ruler of my fief, I became a watcher with many eyes, a listener with many ears, a hider in shadows wearing soundless shoes to spy out the wonders of the bizarre, multitongued worlds of my subjects. Along with my magnificence, the royal right to admire and to despise (always with a touch of condescending affection), I lived with fear, fear that seemed to have been with me almost at birth—and possibly at or before birth, when I had to be dragged forcibly out of the maternal waters. The early wordless fear found causes as I grew older, the causes intertwined with guilt: I must be doing something bad to inspire fearsome happenings. There was the fear of a class door opening to the stony white presence of the school nurse who would find nits in my hair; the fear of losing track of my other skin, my brother; the fear of dropping my baby sister as I carried her down the stairs to her pram; the fear of Tony the barber, who cut my hair with one hand as he stroked me under a big, wide, concealing sheet with the other; and the fear of my father's voice, which could thunder against the walls as his furies drove him. Where *was* my fault? Fault there must be.

There was nothing to do with the fears but give them a companion courage, a courage that early learned slyness and exasperating silence, silence that enraged my father, who liked shrieking combat, his way of yowling at the fates that had made him—a princeling in his mother's household in a small Polish town and an attractive grand seigneur who lived for two blissful New York years unhampered by a wife or children—a factory slave, a Jew slave in a city that rubbed wops and niggers and micks against his singularity. My mother, from whom I had learned the vengeful strength of silences, understood mine, and tacitly approved of them. I was her defiance of the gods that had brought her from an amusing and lucrative career in Warsaw to scrubbing floors and peeling potatoes in a provincial place called the Bronx. It was from her, her determination to attend daily English classes in the local library and to meet with her mandolin group one night a week in spite of my father's sour remarks, that I began to know the face of courage that was independence.

Although she fed me the courage to meet them, the fears didn't leave, they only changed masks: the nurse's face became the face full of harsh words of a boy for whom I was ready to throw myself under a truck; Tony the barber changed to a neighbor who took me to the movies, bought me a candy bar, and wasted his money and much gasping breath doing battle with my tight bra and the tight elastic of my panties.

Gradually, imperceptibly, I became an ally of my fear, using it as a measure of my capacity to endure and combat confrontations with my unhappy, wrathful father. Our major battleground was his vaulting ambition for me to become a concert pianist. He insisted on endless hours of practice, smearing with loathing that which I might have enjoyed were his insistence less. He poisoned my Sunday afternoons by dragging me to the pupil concerts of ambitious local teachers, emphasizing the fact —he swore it was a fact—that the young performers didn't waste their time in school but practiced eight to ten hours a day. I hated them, I hated him, I hated his dream of our future, he as the splendid impresario—as elegantly top-hatted and white-gloved as a picture I had seen of Diaghilev—accompanied by the genius prodigy, his own young daughter. In glorious hotel suites hung with velvet drapes we would lead a life of celebrity, of adulation, of silk shirts and dresses and handmade shoes (reminders of his privileged youth). The fantasies, expressed on long forced after-supper marches, had a bit of the charm of living in the movies, when they weren't chillingly wild. And I was afraid to protest until I was assaulted by a realization that he had erased the rest of my family—my mother, my brother, my sister, obliterated, killed. Though I had long been convinced that, like much of the world, he was mad, this was menacing madness. When his dreams were at their richest and wildest my father bought a reconditioned piano to replace the worn-out calliope I had been using, a deeply threatening act out of a man who was slow with three cents for an ice-cream cone, a gesture that surely meant I would be forced to leave school and live my days chained to the piano. Finally I summoned the courage to scream through my layers of scared silence, "No! No! and No!" The just-like-new piano was not touched for many years.

It was a fearsome act, which would mean enduring the towering, steady rage of my humiliated father, and how would I continue to protect myself? Still, I had won the first major victory of my life, that sweetened by several other triumphs. I could boast to the younger girls of my first menstrual period. My mother celebrated the event by making a dress for me that had a waist and darts under the breasts rather than the shapeless pongee sailor dress that hung loosely from my shoulders year after unchanging year. Now there was a boy who followed *me,* languishing for a pleasant word from *my* scornful face.

With these strides in status, these streams that fed vanity and confidence, I abandoned my infantile rule of the country of Lafontaine. Its subjects had become less mysterious and engaging, they had no more information about sex and birthing to give me and my adroit eavesdropping. My boundaries of school, library, movies, and home had become too tight, like outgrown shoes. I needed new shoes, maybe with shining high heels, and new streets to try them out on: frightening, alluring streets paced by exotic strangers who would have many things to teach me. Packing a bundle of fear, courage, and practiced stubbornness, I was readying for exploration. Not just yet; there would be forests to wander in and tall walls to climb, as in most brave stories; but the need and the right time would meet, I knew, and I could wait, ripening with them.

1. JAMES MONROE H.S.

I am thirteen and a half, graduating from elementary school and hoping to go to high school. It was a rite of passage that would call for light rejoicing, especially in the houses of immigrants, to whom eight years in elementary school meant a long and broad education. In our house, my mother expressed her approbation by buying me a rose, my brother treated me with a modicum of respect on that day, my five-year-old sister beamed at me, so smart and big and the cause of an extra ice-cream cone. For my father it was a day of silent rage, staring at me, staring at the new piano.

If I insisted on going on to high school, he said at supper, it would be only for one more year, a year in which I would study typing and stenography to prepare me for the job that would wipe out—and it would take years—my enormous debt, the piano. Cocooned in guilt from the earliest time, the time when I could walk and my rachitic brother couldn't, I had taken on accretions of additional guilts, like huge warts. You have to respect and love your father; I didn't. You must never lie; I did. You mustn't play doctor; I had. And here stood the greatest guilt, the mountainous one of the new piano, the biggest, most glistening, most expensive, most accusing thing in the house. Because I knew how much the money meant to him, and the glory and future riches it symbolized if only I were a good daughter and used my talents profitably, the piano became a dry, sharp pain in my throat, as if I were being punished with laryngitis because I had silenced the piano.

Here I stand, hobbled in a sack of doom, determined to tear out of it, knowing that I will. There is no clear direction to follow in the welter of impractical ideas that storm my naive mind; nothing but rocklike determination, chiseled and honed to serve as armor and weapon. I keep hoping and looking for clarity in a world that heaps complexity on confusions. The paths opening to clear light under the bowers of bewilderments remain sparse and evanescent. Much, much is sensed, almost learned, but what does it mean, how does it mesh together, if at all?

My voice returned, that of the piano did not, while I struggled with new puzzles in a country entirely foreign to me. Although I had begged to be allowed to go to a general high school, where they taught biology, history, and writing book reports, my father insisted I enter a commercial high school, where the concentration was on office subjects, with classes in English and one foreign language. This with the constant reminder that I would leave at the end of my first year. I didn't know whether he could legally yank me out of school at fourteen and I didn't care after a short while. Nothing could be more depressing than these classes in which I was mud-stupid. My fear of numbers reduced me to idiocy in the bookkeeping class, the finger dexterity the piano had taught me confused my typing. Anger and resistance helped make an utter idiot of me, except in English. I was the best in the class and not too bad in German, my accent sharp mimicry, my vocabulary often reshaped Yiddish.

As the school year was approaching its end, the warnings to look for a job accelerated. How did one get a job at fourteen, and with no skill? I could probably handle a job at the five-and-ten, but most of the employees there were grown women. Where does one begin? Whom to ask? How? If I was asked questions, could I answer? Would I be struck dumb? Would I fall off the edge of the world? Maybe it would be easier to leave home and make money, like pretty, painted, and high-heeled Carola Polanski. But too frightened to apply for a job, how could I hang around street corners and make friends with strange men?

Came an extraordinary event, a miracle worked by exalted personages. My father received a letter signed by my English and German teachers and the principal. It said politely and firmly that I was in the wrong school, that a girl of my interests and capabilities should be offered the broader education of a general high school which might prepare her for college. No one could deny the authority of a high school principal and my father agreed that I be transferred to James Monroe, a new school with an unusually permissive curriculum.

My father's reminders at the end of each semester that I say good-bye to friends and teachers—that was enough school, get a job—helped shape an erratic program for which I have been forever grateful. Since the ordinary stream of studies that answered college requirements were not for me (although I was determined to stay, no matter the cost in effort and quarrels), my courses, other than those absolutely required, were a set of improvisations. First off, no math was demanded, none at all, the school's most bountiful gesture for one blinded by the simplest combination of numbers. Instead, a music course, where I first heard "This is the symphony that Schubert wrote but never finished"—the very short version of elementary school —in its truncated entirety, and a lovely piece of weaving that was a Brahms quartet. An essay on the differences among the Beethoven symphonies earned me a startling compliment from the teacher, a swift little woman who swooped close to the phonograph like a plump hawk when a particular phrase or combination of instruments possessed her and, impelled by her passion, possessed us. She suggested, after having read the Beethoven essay, that I become a music critic. I was pleased but not impressed, since I seemed to be able to knock off an essay on almost any subject easily and fairly well. At any rate, being a music critic was too remote for a girl who had it dinned into her that Jewish goals had to be modest and those of a Jewish woman more modest still.

The English Department, small, talkative, dedicated, maternal, held me in its collective eye, particularly after I had, as a midterm essay, done a small (and, they said, original and pioneer) work on the street cries, the ballads, the game songs of the Bronx, a work I was urged to continue by the head of the department, Mr. Brandon. Any work sustained and slow was, however, too much like practicing the piano to master a late Beethoven sonata. I had no time for step-by-step projects; the urgent need was for swift voyages, with short stops at many ports of call.

James Monroe was the first stage on which I created of myself a distinctive, conspicuous character. My ears had been pierced by my grandmother in Poland when I was a few months old—to preserve my vision, she said. The little turquoise earrings disappeared in America—I suspect my mother's hand. By poking at my earlobes with pins and toothpicks, I opened the old punctures, and with the money I earned teaching six- and seven-year-olds to play the piano, at twenty-five cents a lesson, I bought a pair of Spanish hoops, to become the only girl in school who then had pierced ears, and the fitting Gypsy earrings. The Bergsons, for whom I had become mother's helper during my fourteenth summer, and later on baby-sitter, offered me discarded clothing, my favorites a long dark-gray raincoat and an ancient dark-gold Borsalino hat, the hat of actors and writers. To complement the dark coat and the hat like Renaissance velvet, I bought, out of earnings from teaching old foreign ladies English, two pairs of black cotton stockings and black sneakers. In my earrings, my romantic hat, my slightly sinister coat and black stockings, I could not be mistaken for anyone else in the world. Nor was there any other girl who acted Hedda Gabler in a drama class, twisting a long string of borrowed wooden beads very symbolically and smoking cigarettes, nervously, expertly, throughout the performance, spoken in a voice of sinuous evil.

The indulgent English Department loved all of its promising children with a springtime faith, to the point of freeing them from ordinary curriculum rigidities. Thus some of us were excused from the routine English classes and permitted to gather as poetry groups, as drama classes, as classes in Shakespeare, and I had permission to attend them all. Mr. Brandon, whom I loved as I should have liked to love my father, also invited us to after-school lectures on several subjects. I remember still a lecture on Oriental rugs, illustrated by examples from his own collection, describing their provenances, their variety of weaving techniques, and the meanings in their patterns. He remains one of my immortals, my Marco Polo in Samarkand and Istanbul, the guide to whom I owe the first radiance of Shakespeare sonnets, the flight into Keats's "Eve of St. Agnes," Wilde's dazzle of words and of countless designs and colors that made my eye happy.

The rest of the teaching staff, other than the music and English departments, remain blanks, except for two German teachers and a redheaded vixen in the French Department. One German teacher, Dr. Mankiewicz (an ancestor, I believe, of the movie eminences of that name), was the prototype of the well-padded, easy, philosophic German. When the repetitions of *aus, ausser, bei, mitt, nach, zeit, von, zu* (I think) grew unbearable, I would take a library book out of my bundle and, placing it on my lap, read and read. Once he caught the cast-down eyes in my entranced face and called me and the book to the front of the room. I wasn't afraid, no one was; the atmosphere was of a kindly tolerance just this side of indifference. He asked me what I was reading with such rapture. It was a Knut Hamsun novel; as Dickens and Chekhov had been earlier, Hamsun was my then current bible. Dr. Mankiewicz said my taste wasn't bad, but couldn't I try to learn a little German grammar between the Hamsun paragraphs, as an act of politeness, if nothing else? The other German teacher, Dr. Huebner, who became one of the heads of language studies in the city's schools later on, was beautiful, as precisely featured as a Gothic carving, but unlike those dour knights and saints, he smiled a lot, teaching us a good deal of German by way of songs and simpleminded jokes. So we sang and laughed and earned high Regents' Exam scores for Dr. Huebner.

Miss Ricco lived in a room hung with a huge map of France and a tricolored chart of its cheeses and wines. During the first session she made me take off my distinguished hat and romantic cloak, and continued to gaze at me with suspicion in her raisin eyes. Like the music teacher she was a swooper, not out of enthusiasm but through dislike and boredom. A spinster in her later forties, she had probably been teaching elementary French grammar for too many years, and although sympathy for adults, unless they were run over, or murdered, or something conspicuously bloody like that, was not yet an active ingredient of my adolescence, I was a bit sorry, when I bothered to think about it, that her life was so repetitious and angry. She disliked us all, and any misstep in the mazes of irregular verbs elicited a small, frowning shriek which blew all the verb forms out of our heads, leaving us dumb and empty until the bark of *"Asseyez-vous"* returned us to momentary safety. Between verbs and practice in the placing of slippery little *en*, we read the fables of La Fontaine and were required to memorize and recite one. Mine turned out to be *"La Cigale et la Fourmi."* The recital, from the front of the room to thirty or so students, was impressive. My charlatan vocal cords and mouth, which could shape many sorts of sounds, produced a most elegant accent. Anyone who could play Hedda Gabler had no trouble with the pathos in the voice of the improvident grasshopper: *"Se trouva fort dépourvue / Quand la bise fut venue,"* and the harsh, puritanical command, arm extended like a Calvinist reformer: *"Vous chantiez? . . . Dansez maintenant!"* It was a splendid performance and even Miss Ricco seemed satisfied; it was so splendid, in fact, that I scorned all other work in French and flunked the course, a shocking injustice. How could one humiliate Sarah Bernhardt because she stumbled occasionally on the stupid pebbles of the *plus-que-parfait*? Fortunately, I no longer had to present report cards for parental signatures, and in any case, I was rarely at home and not talking much to anyone there, certainly not about flunking a course, no great matter since I had no interest in accumulating grades for college admission—not for me.

Home was now a workers' cooperative in which my father had invested his savings, on the edge of the upper reaches of Bronx Park, cornering Allerton Avenue, a burgeoning area in the northeast Bronx. Between Lafontaine and Allerton there had been a short stop in an apartment near West Farms, of which I remember only two things: it seemed dark everywhere, even close to a sunny window; and one Saturday afternoon a nice, shy fat boy came to call for me to go to the movies and was so thoroughly questioned by my father about which movie were we going to? when would he bring me home? did he go out with girls much? what did his father do for a living? what were his expectations for a job when he graduated from high school? that the boy suddenly rose, said "Excuse me," and left. It had probably become too late for afternoon prices and the boy was not ready by many years for paternal inquisitions. I left shortly after, scorning my father's "Where are you going? To meet him outside, I suppose," and walked for hours, making sure not to return until ten o'clock, avoiding a spate of questions by locking myself in the bathroom.

For a time I enjoyed the "coops," as the new houses were called. Our apartment was light and fresh and the atmosphere as impassioned in its own way as that of Lafontaine Avenue, my childhood street. This was to be Utopia, a workers' Utopia, run justly and lovingly, truly democratically. It was culturally avid, education of all sorts organized before the last toilets were placed in the bathrooms. There were dance classes, classes in Russian, in English, in political science, in crafts. There was a cafeteria that served huge Jewish-kitchen portions with generous slabs of bread and side orders of pickles and beet salad. There was a large food shop, run cooperatively, to which I refused to go after a comrade clerk laughed at me when I asked for Oscar Wilde sardines. I should have asked for King Oscar but hated him for correcting me, although my error proved the superior quality of my thoughts. In time the food store failed, partially as a result of excessive democracy: a committee of cutters, bookkeepers, and Yiddish journalists, in spite of—or because of—their lengthy discussions, failed to catch the freshest crates of spinach at the most advantageous prices, were bilked by capitalist canned soup suppliers, and blamed each other for costly errors. The cafeteria closed; too many disputes among the cooking comrades, the serving comrades, the cleaning-up comrades, and prices didn't stay idealistically low.

In spite of difficulties and disappointments, spirits stayed high and hot. Rent strikes in the neighborhood were signaled by a banging on apartment doors. "Come! Out! Run! Leave everything, the cossacks [cops] are here!" Whether they wanted to or not, many ran, not always sure they knew where or why, especially the unenlightened housewives caught elbow-deep in washtubs or frying the delicate, perishable crepes of blintzes. Others, always at the ready, dashed with revolutionary fervor. My mother never responded. She said the women who did were *"mishigoyim"* looking for excitement, anything to get away from their sinks and kids. She might have been somewhat right. The children of the most vigorous rent-strike militants, the most insistent shouters and bangers on doors, were the shabbiest, most neglected children, free of bourgeois traits like socks that matched and regular meals. They were often renamed, to their bewilderment, from Solly, Benny, Davy, to Lenin, Marx, Trotsky, which, with the addition of the inescapable diminutive, became Leninel, Marxele, Trotskele. Their mothers, married to the same passive husbands for twenty years, redesigned their lives as well; now members of a new world, they discarded the word "husband" and spoke of their bland men as "mein comrade"—a stormer of barricades, the bearer of the reddest banner.

Observing this noisy, optimistic, unreal life was entertaining

and touching, but other than playing the piano for a dance class
once, I was not part of it. Life was elsewhere: On the East Side
subway to West Farms, picking up a discarded copy of the *World*
and living with its savants and wits. The news was of minimal
interest, but the shining icicle sentences of Alexander Wooll-
cott, balanced by Heywood Broun's good-natured twisting of
humanity's ear, F.P.A.'s rhymed, witty gems, and Frank Sulli-
van's sweet cockeyed world, made me feel, as Erasmus said of
his time, that I was living in a golden age. Then off the subway
at West Farms and a long walk through wide, empty grounds,
spiked with brambles, in my mind the place where Eustacia Vye
met the reddleman. Then a still, scummy canal leading to un-
ambitious Starlight Amusement Park, yearningly lonely early in
the day. Here and there, a tattered Gypsy tent with a hand-let-
tered sign that signaled MIND READER. Was it a promised blossoming, this conglomeration of dull earth and water and tacky
bits of brightness, or was it dying, or both? I never could decide,
was never there in the night blooming of the amusement park,
if blooming there was. It was a curious, stimulating walk; threatening, pleasing, and with its brooding Hardy atmosphere, not
yet gone from my mind.

After school, when we didn't have jobs to go to, a few of us
hung around in the cellar of Harry's house, meant to be a
fashionable "playroom," actually a zoo of bulky old things
Harry's mother couldn't bear to discard: a fat, misshapen couch
burbling stuffing, a porch chair with a sagging cotton bottom
like a full diaper. This was our Florentine academy, our sitting
room in Oxford, our Montparnasse café where Zola met his
painter friends—the place for our discussions of Life and related matters. Religion *was* a drug, we agreed with the savants
who said so. The Pre-Raphaelites painted pictures suitable to
school auditoriums, but the pink, nude frankness of Renoir—
that was real, pertinent. Trotsky really should have succeeded
Lenin; it was his right as proponent of World Revolution. Was
John Dos Passos more class conscious that Upton Sinclair? And
what about Dreiser and Sinclair Lewis? Hell, they were social

critics but not devoted to the suffering poor like the great Dostoevski. "Dostoevski? A religious zealot and archconservative."
"You're crazy." We spoke, of course, much of love and sex,
gleaning most of our wisdom from Havelock Ellis, from dirty
jokes, from a rare page of pornography, from someone's elder
brother's medical books, and from Krafft-Ebing's confusing
revelations about people who were wildly, sexually in love with
shoes. Virgin and eager as we three or four were, we were
afraid of sex and there were few gestures among us, except
when I happened to be alone with robust, direct Harry, who, on
the principle that no red-blooded man alone with a female
would pass up a pass, did a bit of poking and embracing. I didn't
entice him enough to persist when I said, "Cut it out." He did.

Fred, stork-legged and bound in significant silences, was dedicated to poetry and reviled "the double-backed beast" (he was
always finding the sharpest phrases in Shakespeare, like "the
astonished flesh" to go with a bleeding knuckle) that crazed
man's bestial mind. He as school poet and I as master of prose
were linked by our friends and our romantic English teachers.
He was frightened by my vigorous 130 pounds of blond flesh,
or simply disliked me, and I was frightened by the mysterious
cynical thoughts behind his Byronic frown, so we avoided each
other when we could and looked abstractedly high-minded
when we couldn't.

During one semester, a sophisticated, elderly stranger, maybe
eighteen, began to visit the cellar on Harry's invitation. Ralph
was extraordinarily handsome, with keen, shining, narrow eyes
in a dark, sharp face, like a jeweled scimitar. He made contemp-
tuous judgments about our writing—he was writing too, but
wouldn't say what, except that it had nothing to do with dumb
class essays and school-magazine poems—and our naïveté about
sex; virgins, masturbators, all of us. To hell with pouncing
Harry and anemic Fred, this *man* was for me. He was a prize
catch who certainly must be a better guide to sex than our
abominable boarder, my would-be rapist of some years before.
In the breathless competition for Ralph, the man of the world,

my advantages were few but significant. There were infinitely better-looking girls in school and girls with more experience, accumulating a harried something of a sex life on family couches when their parents were out. But not one of them had a room of her own, as I frequently did. The Bergsons, for whom I baby-sat, would take off for occasional amorous weekends of their own, to be undisturbed by the night calls of their two children. I had a room, two rooms, plenty of rooms, when they went away, and I let it be known: "Dammit, rattling around alone again in that big apartment in Greenwich Village"—the absolutely irresistible name, the place of Art and occult adult magics—"with only two sleeping kids for company." It took, as it had to. At ten o'clock one night, after the children had been fed and read to, and had sipped their innumerable delaying drinks of water, Ralph tapped at the door. I let him in. Neither of us knew what to say except "Hello." Neither of us knew what else to say, my Persian prince dwindled to skinny young, I, Village denizen, to shy dope. I hung up his coat, asked him if he wanted something to eat, had he ever eaten French goat cheese? there was some in the icebox. He wasn't hungry, thanks. Like a hired guide, I walked him systematically through the library and pointed out its many volumes in French and German. I took him through the salon to point out the paintings, modern, original. I showed him the two large, shining bathrooms with separate shower stalls. I pointed out the copper molds in the kitchen and explained the Chinese woks. My voice grew flatter and flatter as I showed him Dr. Bergson's initialed silver hairbrushes and his silver shoehorn and the delicate old Kangra painting on the wall.

When the tour was over we stood at the door of the living room, each searching for a helpful phrase. I could summon nothing; he supplied the expected "Wonderful place." Nothing else to do, he grabbed and kissed me, hard, like a stamping machine, and began to pull me away from the living room, not quite sure which direction he wanted. I hadn't imagined that he would sweep me up in his arms while I trailed a long silken scarf, like Gilbert taking Garbo, but I had hoped for some grace and suavity, maybe subtle gestures and slow fire. It was obviously up to me, so I led him, with my limp attempt at grace and suavity, into my bedroom and there we stood, I hoping for melting words, tender nibblings, impassioned embraces or facsimiles. Instead, we seemed to be actors who had forgotten their lines. Teasingly, coquettishly, I thought, I undid the many buttons of the long Oriental silk gown I had borrowed from Laura Bergson's closet. Ralph undressed bumpily, his belt buckle clanging on the bedpost, the buttons on his pants nervously eluding his fingers. We didn't undress altogether, blatant visible nudity beyond our daring. We hastily leaped under the covers in our underclothes. For protection from each other? In the hopes that we would not have to try the awkward act we had ordered of each other? As required, we twisted, stroked, turned, thrusted and folded, slid and kissed, and before I knew what was happening his breath grew hot and gasping and I could feel a warm stream on my belly, long inches from where it should have been.

There was still a long night to go, but we didn't know what to do with it, he stricken by his early ejaculation and in an embarrassed torpor, and virgin I wondering what I had done wrong. Lying flat like two tomb figures, disappointed and worried, we knew nothing to say to each other until, mumbling, "I'm sorry," he dressed quickly, asked which way was out, and was gone. It seemed, I thought, that Ralph didn't know more about techniques than Harry, in spite of his big-shot boasting. Or was there something wrong with me? I wasn't dirty; I had bathed before he arrived and even washed my hair. I didn't stink. Or maybe I did? Maybe I was too fat? Maybe he didn't like the cigarette taste on my mouth. Maybe I had no sex appeal and no one but furtive subway gropers would ever touch me. Maybe I didn't respond properly or enough, maybe I was really a lesbian without knowing it. How did nuns live? Maybe I ought to learn; not convert or enter a nunnery, just find out more about them and their freedom from all this sex trouble.

It was a thick, heavy night and I was relieved to be bothered at dawn by the kids, always difficult when their parents were away overnight. The little girl slapped her spoon spitefully into her cereal, splashing it all over the table and the floor, the little boy hid his potty and, although carefully toilet trained, decided to soil his pants after breakfast. I didn't mind the soiled pants, the floor splotched with cereal, the stomping and shouting of the children. They helped make living more ordinary, more endurable, farther and farther away from the grotesqueries of Ralph and Kate was Antony and Cleopatra.

Ralph stopped coming to our club and shortly left school altogether. Harry's father, who had been threatening for a long time to clean up his cellar and get those damn kids out, finally did. Harry took a job as grocery-delivery boy after school. No more discussions, no more groping, no more club.

2. THE MEN

Ralph gone, Fred floating, Harry and his den preempted, it was essential to find another clubhouse. That was a dark ice-cream parlor in the shadow of the elevated subway tracks on Westchester Avenue, hardly a distinguished place, but it served for the afternoons I was free to meet with a new circle, a very small one. Comparatively well-heeled at the time, I treated to Cokes, although black coffee and a string of cigarettes better suited my more decadent persona. One of us three regulars was lissome, white-skinned Bernie, who liked to wear bright flying scarves and asked that we call him "Bernarr," in the French manner. He and I frequently went downtown on Saturdays to search out cheap matinee tickets at Gray's. These had to be serious, possibly classical, preferably foreign plays. We found everything we saw entrancing, though it was required that we express light scorn of the costumes, or the sets, or the acting, and unless it was Shakespeare, Ibsen, or Chekhov, of the writing. We were laboriously witty and high-flown; we never talked simply with each other, yet were close friends, essential to each other as actor and audience. He was sixteen and I fifteen and, like many adolescents, inhabited an exaggerated Mannerist world of overlarge, shocking volutes alternating with deep niches. We were also tearing away from the restraints of who we

thought we were to the freedoms of who we thought we wanted
to be, trying on a succession of identities. We were palimpsests
of masks, the earliest one, of open-mouthed bewilderment, covered by a questioning, frowning mask and, at the current level,
a thin screen of fake sophistication, uncertainly attached, slipping as it tried to hold to a semblance of imperturbability, of
confidence. (Many years will pass, amorphous adolescence
supposedly long faded, yet shades of the masks will cling, even
into the folds of the shroud. James Joyce: "We walk through
ourselves, meeting robbers, ghosts, giants, old men, wives,
widows. . . ." And Jorge Luis Borges says it as: "among the
forms in my dreams are you—Shakespeare—who like myself
are many and no one.")

A third member of our circle, a portly wearer of fancy waist-
coats and a big, old-fashioned watch chain, was not of the school
and our only explanation for his persistent presence was that he
had seen Bernie in the neighborhood and was courting him.
Derek enhanced the possibilities of homosexual interest in Bernie by being awesomely, lengthily encyclopedic about Hadrian
and Antinoüs, about the Spartan warriors and their devoted
young companions, about Alexander, about Leonardo. In his
languid and vaguely British speech, he would recite long sections of "Reading Gaol" and the brightest conversational
thrusts attributed to Wilde. An odder now and then member of
the club wore a mannish suit and a porkpie hat over a boy's
haircut. She carried a slim volume of verse with always a fresh
rose to mark one poem we were never allowed to see and which
she wouldn't identify. The rose and the poem were an immortal
dedication to one love and muse, she said, a melding of Sappho,
Isadora Duncan, and Colette. She had originally come to search
me out because a mutual friend had told her I wore a golden
Borsalino and black stockings and was in other ways rebellious
and attractive.

At some point I grew tired of the three. The girl reminded
me of John Held, Jr., cartoons of slick-haired, vapid young men,
her appreciation of me became uninteresting, her paeans to the

fair unknown, ultimately boring. She soon returned to her private isle of Lesbos or wherever she had come from. Derek left us shortly after, perhaps for more worldly companions who might be closer to the imagined witty green rooms of London theaters where someone like Bosie might be sitting, maybe waiting for him. Bernie-Bernarr and I continued to hunt out bargain tickets and remained friends, without clinging to each other as before.

A curious "Through the Looking Glass" scrim fell over my life. As the porkpie hat and one perfect rose, as the rosy plump finger on the watch chain, as the flying scarves faded, I was steadily assaulted by shocking, hallucinated smells: of the thick fattiness of entrails on the butcher's block, of the singed chicken feathers in a neighbor's kitchen, of hot roof tar, of the heady metallic odor of menstrual blood, of acrid semen—the smells of sex. Brilliant dreams were the paintings of the smells. The setting of one dream was the laundry in which I ticketed bundles of wash, surrounded by fellow workers who cheered me on as I sat hatching a large egg which would soon produce my baby. They were playful, I was playful; there were no labor pains, no instruments, no swelling, no convulsions, words and images that had filled my childhood with guilt and horror. Though I had several versions of the dream, I never hatched the baby. I sat and talked and was admired and encouraged and there the amusing dream floated away. A less forthright, slyer dream had me walking through sun-dappled birch (birth?) trees wearing a fox around my shoulders, the proud ornament of lower-middle-class women. My fox was handsome, full-bodied, and alive (had I read the Lawrence story?), feeding at my breast. Though he drew a trickle of blood, his gnawing and nibbling didn't hurt at all; it was rather pleasing to have him there, burrowing into my chest. That dream was also very entertaining and still is: the economy of a symbol that suggested so much—nursing, the breaking of the hymen, its trickle of blood. The masterstroke was, I thought, "fox" for "fuck," a word I couldn't get myself to say until much later (it was thoroughly the property of men and boys), and here I made so adroit a pun on the word without having to say it.

Another set of dreams was a total denial of sly foxes and hatching babies; they were romantic and lyrical. I was being softly kissed and gently caressed by a shadowy phantom lover. Always the place was lovely—a meadow of flowers like mille-fleur tapestry, the edge of a dimpled lake, bowers of fruit trees—and always the same denouement: the shadowy lover became flesh. When his ardor began to agitate the delicate languors and the fairy-tale landscape, I would sit up, reach for an apple from the branch curving over my head, and crunch into it vigorously and loudly, or admire extravagantly the strong, rapid head of a woodpecker nearby. The disconcerted lover disappeared and I was left contentedly alone, a pure white blossom not yet plucked, and reluctant, it seemed, to be.

The fox, the birthing, the smells, the dreams preoccupied so openly with sex as yes, sex as no, may have led in some subterranean way to the night of the cat.

While I was foraging in literature and music, biology was becoming interesting as well. The smell of formaldehyde became yet another of my especial odors; the frog splayed out and pinned, his efficient, neatly arranged inner geography suggesting more mysteries to be explored. The boy with whom I shared a dead frog in a shallow baking tin was rather like an early P.S. 58 admirer, shaggy, fetching, and freckled, like a *Saturday Evening Post* boy. The resemblance ended there. Barry was utterly indifferent to me and, seemingly, had no interest in anyone else. He was alone most of the time, a mediocre student except in biology, where he was a wonder. He rarely spoke to me until, under his muttered warnings and imprecations, I had become a fairly skillful dissector. One day he asked me to meet him in the lunchroom, I couldn't imagine why. He offered a troublesome proposal. Since the laundry in which I worked wasn't too far away, and he lived around the corner, why didn't I meet him in the evening, after work, to chase down a cat—there were lots of strays in the neighborhood—which we would chloroform and dissect in his cellar laboratory. Because I liked and respected cats, because I didn't want to kill anything but wanted to know if I could, because I was sure we would be caught by the police and imprisoned for years, because my chest and head pounded "*No!*" I said, laconically, "OK."

We met one evening at about eight o'clock in front of the school and walked into the long spread of my Thomas Hardy emptiness near West Farms. Barry was not a skillful hunter and I was little help, unable to chase or pounce or grab. My best contribution was to menace the cats with a stick, hoping they would run in his direction and he would do the rest. After a discouraging hour he lunged full length at a small gray-striped cat and, with her body pinned under his, slipped a noose around her neck, then pulled her, mewling and choking, to his darkened house. He unlocked the cellar door and dragged the cat down a long flight of wooden stairs that led to an old kitchen table, to jars and cans, scissors and knives and chemical stinks. Out of one of the cans he took a large wad of dirty absorbent cotton, gesturing to me to bring him another container. I didn't know which he meant; I probably didn't want to. He dropped the absorbent cotton, tied the cat with its lasso string to the table, then picked up the dirty wad of cotton and poured a sweet-smelling liquid out of a bottle he recapped quickly. He muttered "Chloroform" as he approached the struggling, shrieking cat. As he held the cotton to her face, her legs churned, her body twisted and trembled under the tight cord. Her tail stretched, lashed, stretched, and dropped. She was quiet. "Start cutting the string from her—there's the scissors, there, on the table." "How do you know she's dead?" "Oh, I'm pretty sure she is, and when we start dissecting she'll die anyhow, won't she?" I had been willing down the vomit that kept rising to my throat. Now it was in my mouth. I ran up the stairs and vomited at the side of the cellar door. Heaving and in a gelid sweat, I rushed to the subway station, sure I would be apprehended for murder any second now, seeing accusation on each face in the street. Everyone in the subway car knew I was a murderess; at the next stop a policeman would take me off the train and drag me to prison. I made it home and to the bathroom, where I vomited again. I heard my father mutter that I was learning to drink, too, with my bum friends, drinking the homemade stuff that made people blind. When my mother asked me what was wrong, I said I must have eaten something rotten in the cafeteria near the laundry, a real greasy spoon.

The terror of being arrested diminished after a week or so, but Barry and I hardly spoke though we still shared the same frog. I never found out if he had actually dissected the cat, never asked, never wanted to know. It was enough to acknowledge that although I had not killed the cat, I had consented to its death. Was I a murderess? Was Barry a murderer? Did everyone conceal a killer? Could be. (The cat stayed with me for decades. During an experiment with hallucinogenic mushrooms in Mexico, many years later, the cat returned as myself, my brain scrambled as hers must have been under the chloroform: sounds became visual images and what I saw was tapped out in rhythmic sounds while I made mewling, strangled attempts to talk, to protest, to stay alive.)

The springtime of that year stayed clouded by the dead cat, and all of school, everything in it, even the English and music classes, became loathsome. Morning after morning, I would approach the red-brick school building with its dead doors and brutal hinges, turn back to the subway, which took me to Grand Central and the majestic lions and stairs of the "big library" at Forty-second Street and Fifth Avenue. No one questioned students in those days and I had the royal privilege—a most adult privilege—of going through the immensity of card files, submitting slips for books, and when my number showed at the delivery desk, carrying my treasures to a dignified chair under a dignified lamp. Here I stayed throughout the day, reading Robinson Jeffers, Robert Frost, T. S. Eliot, and Ezra Pound, poets whom I didn't always understand but whose company flattered me, as did the company of my serious, elderly, learned neigh-

bors, who permitted me to breathe of the cultivated atmosphere
that was theirs.

This idyll of freedom and respect, of politeness and dedication to learning, lasted about two months, until I was called to
the assistant principal's office and shown that I had cut school a
shocking number of days, without a note from my mother or a
doctor to justify the absences, and that I had attended only one
gym class during the semester. That day my faithful double, the
me who stood off observing while I acted, burst into laughter
when I assumed the grotesque position—ass out, face pushed
stupidly forward—for swinging a baseball bat. So I decided to
skip the whole nonsense and started for the door, still laughing.
The stout gym teacher, infuriated by my insouciance and laughter, called me back and began to push at my legs for their
proper planting in the baseball stance and to pull my arm into
the approved bend for wielding a bat. I wouldn't and couldn't
obey and she began to shout at me. Suddenly I began to cry,
loudly and heavily, and sank like a sack—the bat rolling away
from me—to the floor, to sit there sobbing. I was playacting
and yet not altogether: confusion about the cat and fear of the
results of my present lawlessness, a mist of unhappiness that
enclosed me when I was not in my library, were authentic in-
gredients of the theatrics.

I would flunk the gym course, the assistant principal said, and
possibly others, and would be handled as a truant, constantly
watched. Not quite ready to be expelled, I cut down my pure,
serene days downtown but continued to avoid gym classes, Ne-
anderthal pleasures.

In spite of the thickheaded school authorities, the melancholy
fogs that touched me, life gradually became multistranded and
rich. Having finished dripping rain, the trees began to shed
blossoms; suddenly a yard yesterday fit only for a doghouse
sprang yellow flames of forsythia; my laundry gave me a small
raise, the library job for which the English Department recom-

mended me stayed easy and pleasant. The apogee of that singing, dancing springtime was my acquisition of two suitors. They
were in their late twenties, not boys, men, and close friends. Joe
was a short, barrel-chested man with a droll, lopsided face. He
had a mean job, dull bread-and-butter hours between happy
lunch breaks which he spent searching out second-hand records
on Sixth Avenue stalls: one movement of a Mahler symphony,
Chaliapin singing "The Song of the Flea," Rosa Ponselle singing "Pace, Pace"—a little scratched on one side but wasn't she
gorgeous? Evenings he took high school classes to prepare for
City College extension courses. His Sundays were fiestas of
pleasures: the Lower East Side early in the morning to look for
more cheap records, then tennis in some free park court or
other, and in the evening, visiting friends, playing his balalaika
to Russian songs—longing for birch trees and half-forgotten
villages—robustly roaring the beauties of "Kalinka."

His host on many Sunday evenings was Mark, who looked like
Marcel Proust, hooded dark eyes and sadness to the bone.
Mark's family lived immediately below mine in the "coops."
Since I spent little time there, I didn't encounter him for some
time after we had moved in. Or possibly I paid him no attention,
assuming he was one of the local young fathers. It was my
mother who told me, when I stood still long enough to listen,
that the woman downstairs, Mrs. Rosinsky, a talker with a
bunched-up face, claimed to have been rich in Russia, before
the Bolsheviks took her house and her husband's business. The
jewels she had hidden in her skirt hem fed the family, two sons
and herself (the husband seemed to have disappeared), as they
made their long way to Shanghai, and slowly, after years, to
America. Could I believe such a story, with lots of strange details she didn't remember? It didn't matter whether the story
was true or not; people who could invent such a tale—if they
did—were worth knowing, and then there were the alluring
Russian songs that stretched themselves on long, sad chords of
nostalgia from their window to ours. How I got to know
stricken-faced Mark Rosinsky I don't remember, but I some-

how managed it and soon was a frequent Sunday evening visitor, petted and spoiled by friend Joe. To celebrate a minor school achievement, Joe gave me a record of a Schubert piano sonata played by Alfred Cortot. He tried to teach me to play tennis, but anything I couldn't do well immediately I wouldn't do at all; too much exposure of gracelessness and ineptitude, a painful display of frailties that were to be kept hidden. The lessons trailed off. So he took me to the Lower East Side on record hunts and taught me a few Russian songs. It was Joe who managed to get to the Lewisohn Stadium early enough to buy (Mark always included) the twenty-five-cent concert seats, and it was Joe who knew friendly Carnegie Hall ushers who let us climb, for fifty cents, often for nothing, to seats in the top balconies. Being with funny-looking Joe was light and laughter, too often clouded by Mark's silent darkness. During my short tennis career, Mark had stood at the side and watched me scoop at the ball and miss it, fall over my own feet, serve in wild, unexpected directions, every awkward mishap made more hideous by his fixed, critical gaze.

He wasn't appraising me critically, it began to appear. He kept the door to his apartment open so he might rush to the door to greet me when he heard my footsteps. At unexpected times, I would find him standing at the subway station, ready to walk back to the "coops" with me. At other unexpected times —when he should long have been at work—I would find him at the foot of our staircase asking politely if he couldn't escort me to the subway. I lied wildly in several directions simultaneously. No, thanks; I was going to walk to the library this morning. No, thanks; there were no classes and I was going to visit a sick friend. No, thanks; I had to do an errand for my mother. No, thanks. No, thanks. But he found me going up, going down, going out. The solemn face and voice became importunate, distorted in his urgency. Why couldn't we meet alone? He had important things to say to me that were not Joe's business. He would take me to a theater, or a concert, or a nice restaurant downtown. It wasn't so much to ask, was it, to go out with him

alone, to talk? He wouldn't touch me, he would do anything I
wanted. He would try, if we got to be real friends, as I was with
Joe, to get me a room of my own, which, he knew, I so much
wanted. That would come in time, though. First, please, please,
let's spend a few hours together and let me tell you how I feel
about you.

One night when I found him at the bottom of the stairs of the
subway station, I began to run and he to run after, pleading
breathlessly. I felt choked, sick, tormented; I could neither understand nor meet this thing that tortured and drove him. It
was not a crush as I knew them, goggle-eyed and mute. This was
love, grown-up and terrible, and I had done it to him, as if I had
actually crippled or blinded him. I was netted, trapped in this
ring of fire I had set unwittingly for both of us. Feeling as much
a victim as he—or was this torture pleasure for him?—I wanted
him away, out of my sight, out of my life. The following Sunday,
when I knew he would be at home, with many opportunities to
wait and listen for me in his patient, suffering way, I hitchhiked
to the place, an hour or so from the city, where I had a friend
with whom I could shelter for the day. I found her reading and
bored and we decided to walk to the village grocery, where we
might find other friends. As we approached the store, at the
main crossroads of the village, the bus that connected with the
train from the city stopped. Off stepped Mark. I ran, I don't
remember where, or where I hid that day, or how and when I
got back. Under the door at home I found his note: "You don't
have to run away from me anymore. I won't bother you again."

My inability to cope with Mark, the sense of undefined and
undeserved guilt I felt toward him, did not impair fun with Joe,
but rather enhanced it. For one thing, Mark was afraid of Harlem, and now Joe and I were free to attend rehearsals of the
Hall Johnson Choir, to which Joe had, as was his habit, gracefully wangled an invitation from someone he happened to meet
and charm. We went to German and Russian restaurants—
cheap, the cheapest and most generous those of the national
homes, community centers that offered legal advice, ward heel-

ing, sociability, lessons in English, dancing, and unfamiliar foods at minute prices to members and guests of various immigrant communities. Our favorites were the Polish National Home, near McSorley's on Seventh Street, whose bowls of food danced on the tables to polka rhythms one tin ceiling above; and the Bohemian National Home, uptown, which decorated itself with peasant motifs in unabashed colors and with blond, very white-skinned, Art Nouveau women, the women who still sing the heroines in *The Grand Duchess of Gérolstein* in Budapest, the type that later became known to us as the Gabors.

It was Joe who introduced me to Dr. Caligari's Cabinet, his cubist ashen makeup and his sinister gloves and broken hat. Joe told me Charlie Chaplin was a comic genius and I believed him but resisted Chaplin films because I had wept through all of *The Gold Rush* when I was a little girl and was wary of having little Charlie tear me to bits again. On overtime pay we went to a small Russian nightclub on Fourteenth Street near Second Avenue, where men in wide-skirted cossack coats glided swiftly on their toes like ballet dancers and threw knives around each other; exciting, foreign, *muy macho*. Across from the nightclub (was it called The Two Guitars? The Three Guitars? The Balalaika?) was a Jewish restaurant as sweetly solicitous and talkative as the national homes, and as cheap.

Chronology, an elusive, slippery thread of my memory, leaves me uncertain as to whether or not it was Joe who introduced me to early Russian movies; I think it was. At any rate, it was in his time that I saw the landmark *Potemkin*, whose rushing masses meant nothing to me because, although I had heard of Soviet Russia as the new Utopia, I knew nothing of its historical facts. One beautiful, sadly exotic film was *Gypsies*, so moving and impressive that I still remember, over the span of decades, the tune of one lovely melancholy song. Other Russian films seemed to be concerned with people in love with tractors, condensed for me as one large woman, significantly pregnant, standing in profile before a crude farmhouse at the edge of endless wheat fields full of tractors, and calling in a shattering voice to an unseen, faraway comrade, "K-O-O-O-lya-a-a."

At one rock-bottom financial stage Joe found us a ten-cent movie house, under the Third Avenue El, one of those dim, tattered houses that spread their aisles and toilets with perfume like melted lollipops to disguise the smell of past and present urine. Joe muttered apologies, but I didn't care; this dump was like the five-cent Lyric Theater on Third Avenue near 180th Street, where my brother and I sat entranced, oblivious of perfume and urine, watching Elmo Lincoln cut off the outlaws at the pass. Joe's dump was showing a version of *Camille* with Nazimova and Rudolph Valentino, in my recollection a vast bed of lacy pillows, nervously quivering nostrils, heaving chests, and a surrealist excess of long, narrow-eyed, staring passion.

It was Joe, with friends everywhere, who introduced me to the freezing tenement studios on the East River later torn down for the U.N. enclave, and to the big misshapen houses in Hoboken, reached by ferry from the end of Christopher Street, not yet the "meat market" it would later famously become. Like Mr. Brandon at James Monroe, Joe was one of my Marco Polos, leading me into many realms and holding forth, as future forays into Cathay, night walks through the Fulton Fish Market and maybe boarding one of the Portuguese fishing boats swaying under the Brooklyn Bridge. He had a friend . . .

Although Mark kept his promise not to bother me, not to trap me on the stairs, not to trap me at the station, not to trap me at all, his mother remained a nuisance via my mother, who was amused while I was both annoyed and amused. The little woman came almost daily to tell my mother that Mark could not support a wife yet, not for a long time; his job paid too little. She had a lot of medical expenses and needed a whole set of new teeth, and although the younger brother had a part-time job, they had to help support him through two more years at City College. And didn't my mother think me much too young for marriage or even being engaged? Though I was a big, well-developed girl who looked and acted older than my age, I was, we all realized, only fifteen and we weren't Old Country peasants who married their daughters off so young, were we? My mother and father surely had higher ambitions for me than her Mark, a poor workingman. I was so brilliant I could marry a doctor or a professor. I was so beautiful I could marry a millionaire. My chances were boundless, and why trample on them now? My mother answered that neither she nor I was interested in marrying me off; that I didn't want a husband, or any man, who would get in my way of finishing high school and maybe—who knows?—college.

Whether the situation I was in, courted by two *men*, not impetuous, ignorant boys, put it in my mother's mind, or my father's, a new suitor was brought in. A family that was distantly related to my family, the Woolfs, who lived in a large house on the edge of Morris Park and were obviously prosperous, had several daughters and one son, Jerry. The son, when I thought of him at all, became a vaguely romantic image; he was a sailor—that impossibly extraordinary thing a Jewish sailor. Nevertheless he had to be a tall, bronzed Viking with keen, far-seeing blue eyes, wearing dashing tatters (there was a touch of the pirate in him, too). It was somehow arranged, probably by my father, that on one of his leave days he come to visit and take me out. I opened the door to a slight man with a pleasant smile, wearing a conventional brown suit, a brown tie, and well-polished brown shoes. After greeting my parents pleasantly, modestly proffering thunderous words—Hong Kong, Nagasaki, Bangkok—in response to their questions, he turned to me and said he had theater tickets for us and maybe we'd better hurry a little.

Conversation was easy. He said he read a lot between ports and he understood that I read a good deal, too. We talked books, I rather impatiently, eager to know about all the places he had been and what they were like. He told me there were beautiful painted caves in India and canals full of floating markets in Bangkok and that the Chinese who hung around the ports were the cleverest traders; you had to watch out for their quick tricks. From Union Square we walked east to a Russian restaurant, where he ordered for me delicious, expensive things, and to cap my delight hailed a taxi—I had never been in one—to take us westward on Fourteenth Street to the Civic Repertory Theater, whose cheap upper seats had taught me every line of Chekhov's *Three Sisters* and Ibsen's *Master Builder*. Now we were sitting in the orchestra, and on the stage was the great Nazimova playing Madame Ranevskaya in *The Cherry Orchard*. So moved was I by Nazimova—the real, actual Madame Ranevskaya, I felt—and by the old servant losing his life with the cherry trees, so moved by being treated like a grown, dignified woman on a grown, dignified date, that I had to sit straight and stiff in my seat, to contain everything that was going on in me. Now and then Jerry smiled at me, as if understanding and enjoying my heady pleasure. After the performance, the courtly acts went on in their classic design: he asked me if I'd like a soda. While I was sipping the unaccustomed nectar, he took a small box out of his pocket and saying, "I brought this for you, I thought you might like it," lifted out of the box a string of light-brown, carved beads. I looked but didn't reach for them. No one ever had given me such a present; hand-me-downs, loans, discards, yes, but not a new special thing of my own. While I hesitated, smiling and dumb, he said, "Smell them. They're carved of sandalwood." I took the string from his hand, put it to my face, and pictures of antelopes and huge flowers in jungle groves and birds of a hundred colors swam through my head. My nice, polite brown Jerry really was, if not a Viking, a world wanderer, an intimate of places whose names I didn't even know, someone who might, were he older, have been a drinking companion of Gauguin in Tahiti.

I was not in love with him—that was our only encounter— but I cherished him and the gala evening. I wrote him sporadically for a number of years, until I overheard Mrs. Woolf's pained voice whispering to my mother that he was settling in Japan with a Japanese wife. The beads remained my most important possession and stayed with me until I began to live in places where things disappeared.

Mrs. Rosinsky took heart when she saw me walking down the stairs with Jerry, but when he didn't reappear she renewed displaying her wounds of concern and banners of praise to my mother, who reported it all to me. That is, when we weren't fighting about my smoking, my erratic eating habits, my crazy, schleppy coat, and—one monumental fight that lasted for hours—Isadora Duncan. I knew she was a great woman, an artist, a heroic world spirit. My mother said she was a bohemian bum who drank too much and had too many lovers, one of them a billionaire, one of them a Bolshevik. I marched out and went to sleep with my friend Minnie, complaining into the night about the vulgar conventionalism, the narrow-minded insensitivity, of my bourgeois mother.

3. THE CHILDREN

The summer following my first year in high school, my mother had announced that she had saved enough money selling corsets—ready-made and those she devised—during our school hours to buy us all a vacation for three weeks. She disliked the clusters of *yachnes* who invaded the rooming houses of the Catskills and fought for space in communal kitchens. She had heard of a farmer not far from the city who had remodeled large chicken houses, put in beds and minute kitchens, and rented them out during the summer. We took off for the full, joyous three weeks of three kids in a bed, a spigot of cold water outside for washing dishes and faces, an outhouse with two holes and a chemical-plus-shit smell and clouds of buzzing large golden flies. And boundless grass to run on, trees to swing from, buttercups and daisies for chains and chaplets. There must have been rain and the discomfort of huddling in the narrow space, but I remember the time as a steady glow of golden sun. Dignity hit me every once in a while—I was still awed by my menstrual periods—and I left my running and leaping brother and sister to wander through the chicken house community and beyond, meeting girls my age who lived near a lake, where I was occasionally invited to swim.

Among our immediate neighbors there were two families I

was smitten with. One consisted of a silent old man, as stiff as a sword under his discolored, swooping Panama hat, and his two silent daughters like swans, floating by us gracefully in splendid discolored linens and gauzes, their hair pulled taut to back knots, like ballerinas. The truth was difficult to find out surely, but these aristocrats, we were told, were a Prince and Princesses Dolgoruky—an ancient noble Russian name—who had escaped Russia during the revolution and were waiting to return to their blue-and-white palace in St. Petersburg when the crazy fury that had seized their country abated. This information came from another neighbor, a stout, heavy-browed Russian woman with a glorious accent, all rippling *r*'s and no "a"s or "the"s among her fast, tumbling sentences. She knew all the names and faces of the Russian aristocracy, and they should burn in hell; those who were still alive, like Dolgorukys, should slowly starve to death while the people's revolution went on to full triumph all over the world, as Trotsky said it had to and would. The lodestar of her life, several shades above Trotsky, was her son of three or four, a fat little brown berry who ran around naked, much to my five-year-old sister's amazement and amusement as his penis dangled and swung—like a pink bell, she said. The child had few companions but his mother; his English was precisely like hers in accent and syntax. He was an engaging, trusting innocent and we fed him Fig Newtons and Lorna Doones surreptitiously (his mother forbade all sweets) under the guise of teaching him to speak more correctly. We thought that learning songs in English would improve his pronunciation. The accent was, however, obdurate and all we got for our pains—no pain at all and for many years an entertaining memory—was a song called "Cvementime," whose chorus, sung musically and with feeling, was "Oo mine dahving, oo mine dahving, oo mine dahving Cvementime—You arrrr vost und gun ferreverrr, oo mine dahving Cvementime." We soon stopped trying to improve his accent; this performance, often repeated at our request, was a perfect thing, not to be marred by correction.

During a walk to the community near the lake a mile or two

away I encountered a girl picking blackberries at the side of the road. As I helped her pick, she asked me if I would like to be a mother's helper the following summer; that is, would I like to live with a nice family named Bergson and take care of their children? The pay wouldn't be much above bed and board, but they were decent about time off and Mrs. Bergson was especially sweet and generous. She herself had to turn the job down because her family was moving out to Detroit, where, her uncle had written, her father might find an auto factory job. I said I was very much interested and, wiping the blackberry stains from my hands and mouth, followed her directions to the proper house. Stammering a little, I told the lady who opened the door that I would like the job, that having taken care of my brother and sister most of my years, I was well experienced in caring for children. She thought I would be satisfactory, the gentle-faced lady said, but in the meantime could I baby-sit in their city apartment once or twice so we could get to know each other and to find out if I really wanted and was suited for the summer job? Of course, and I gave her my name and address and the phone number of a friend who took messages for me.

There was some baby-sitting that following winter, but I did not actually learn the Bergsons and their community until the following summer. The community was a stretch of flat undistinguished land about an hour and a half by train from New York. The original settlers were dissenters of several shades of left—anarchists, socialists, communists, whose assembled weapons were the words of their tutelary gods, Lenin, Trotsky, Emma Goldman, Rosa Luxemburg. On each acre or two of inexpensive land they put, at first, the simplest of bungalows, which, with the years, grew more livable but never wholly "bourgeois." Among the other dissenters there were the vegetarians, and the supervegetarians, who would touch nothing but roots, fruits, nuts, and berries. There were some of no clear political faith except that they despised all Republicans (except Abraham Lincoln) and all Democrats except Franklin Delano Roosevelt and Henry Wallace, who was saving a hungry world with his new strains of strong, fast-growing wheat. Although the majority were Jewish, they named themselves "agnostic" or "atheist," and thought that fasting on Yom Kippur was as barbaric as drinking the blood of Christ at Catholic services. The only passion that, in some, almost resembled religion was the passion for wholesome, whole-grain breads and biscuits, lumpish things weighed down with sincerity and no leavening of skill. One woman with an invisible husband and several zesty children produced an almost palatable loaf and gathered to herself a near-monopoly, bested only by the unbeatable monopoly of the local food shop which sold the great American goody, squeezable, rubbery white bread. Stuck between the impenetrable dark bread with its half-raw grains and the drooping, feeble white slabs, those of us with a taste for palatable bread occasionally hitchhiked into the city to drag back sacks of bagels, seeded ryes, and crusty Italian rolls to be dispensed to friends as payment for favors past and future.

Those who had rejected the artifices of the city completely, the people who endured the winter's cold in poorly heated houses, depending on fireplaces and heavy homemade sweaters for warmth, sent their children to a school the parents devised and established, a free-form school that prized artwork above reading (the playful, bright ten-year-old twins of a master carpenter didn't know how to read at all and their parents didn't seem to care), "freedom of expression" above disciplined learning. It shocked my Bronx public school ear to hear teachers addressed by their first names and parents called "May" and "Harry" by their young, although I approved heartily of this advance in civilization.

As an adjunct to the schoolhouse there was a social hall, large enough to hold a stage and seats for about two hundred people. Although there were occasional appearances by visiting guests who sang or danced in Duncan peplums or recited poetry in English or Russian (Yiddish was rarely heard, a rather despised speech of the stupid Zionists who were dividing an already excessively divided world, which should be united as one universal humane government), young local talent was given its chance. After I had been with the Bergsons for some weeks and become acquainted with some members of the community, I was asked, along with several young musicians, to take part in a recital. I played my stellar achievement—the peak of my capacity in speed, in rubato, in sweet pathos—Chopin's "Fantaisie Impromptu." I had practiced it for many months before I quit practicing altogether, and still played it in friends' houses. It was well in my fingers and memory, and I thought it was going beautifully when I heard a giggle as I played. It may have been meant for me: in my pianism as in my general conduct there were often affectations that were designed to lend me greater probity as a bona fide artist, necessarily eccentric, and I might have displayed some peculiarity in my playing. Although I never tried to change or in any way modify Chopin—the awe was too great and he was, especially as a doomed tubercular like Keats, one of my most moving and enduring loves, a love who sang my nameless yearnings—I may have raised my hand too high in letting a lyric passage float away, as I had seen Ossip Gabrilowitsch do, or bend low to the keys seeming to snuffle among the keys like a hog, as old de Pachmann did. The giggle may not have been attached to my performance at all, but, the great artiste insulted, I rose from the piano halfway through the piece and stalked out, my eyes set on the door, not to look at any face. One girl of my acquaintance, who sat in the audience after performing a Polish folk dance, came after me. They were dopes and didn't know music, and she wasn't going to perform for them again she said as she looked at my stiff face, the shut dimmed window through which no one could see the burning in my veins and entrails. I couldn't cry; I hadn't since I was seven or eight, after I was accused of crying too easily; so I ran in several wild directions until I found myself on the road that led to the Bergsons' house. The children were asleep, the mother about ready for bed. There were no questions or comments after Laura Bergson looked at my deadened face. I couldn't sleep but seethed in anger against the giggler and, more, against myself. Why did I do such a dumb thing? I could play the "Fantaisie Impromptu" without mannerisms and still seem to be an impressive young pianist. What did I think I was doing with the gestures borrowed from anybody who did something I thought looked artistic? Why did I have to try to impress everyone around me with the fact that I was unique? Did I really impress them as special, outside the common herd? Or as crazy?

The cocoon of self-contempt in which I was bound pricked and burned for several days, but I was since early childhood prepared to fulfill prescribed duties no matter how I felt, no matter that I wanted to roll up in a corner to die. Laura, who was genuinely sympathetic and becoming attuned to my moods, didn't ask why I was so quiet. She, too, was preoccupied, polite, silent, and dutiful, as she carried her own sack of pain. I knew that her husband Ivan was not coming up on the following weekend and I had gotten to know him well enough to understand that this was one of his frequent declarations of independence from marriage, a chance to unleash his irresistibility on wider spheres.

Our silences were broken into, gradually, by the needs of the children and by visiting neighbors, several of whom carried petitions to halt the execution of Sacco and Vanzetti, scheduled for late that August. I wasn't sure of just what they had done, but I had been told they were Italian radicals being victimized by the American capitalist establishment. They were undoubtedly innocent; many important people said so; and who didn't know that Boston was the seat of xenophobic, throttling conservatism? Knowing little of the details, I nevertheless aligned myself body and soul with the immigrants and against the natives, a throwback to the Them and We schism innate to the immigrant neighborhood of my childhood. Sacco and Vanzetti were, as well, Italian workers like those I had known intimately; in a sense, close relatives. There was nothing I could do about their situation but go to rallies in the community and, on a day off, give out leaflets in the city. I tried to imagine, for the first time in my life, how it might feel to await certain death, how it actually felt—the buzzing, the piercing, the burning in the body—to be electrocuted in a big, hideous, wired throne, like the murderess Ruth Snyder in the picture in the *Daily News.*

Sacco and Vanzetti's deaths interfered minimally, however, with the last community dance, a farewell among mother's helpers, young masons, and some of the chosen whose families had the money to send them to the University of Wisconsin, an Olympus ruled by a liberal genius-educator named Kirkpatrick, who was freeing his university of the barnacles that hung on most colleges. I was invited to the dance by one of the summer delivery boys, accepted happily, and then regretted having accepted. I was a mediocre dancer and had nothing festive to wear; a small sun blister on my lip looked like a chancre; my hair was wild, sun-bleached and uncontrollable and except for a polite dance or two with my date, who else would guide me to the floor? When I told Laura I wasn't going, she took from her closet a dress of dark rose linen which I had admired and coveted; the wide skirt danced of itself and the deep-cut bodice dangled small silk flowers. "Wear this dress; it will fit you. Tie a ribbon around your hair, put some powder on your blister, and go." I went and felt airy and like poetry in Laura's dress and because I was asked to dance by several boys. I was only lightly bothered by my friend Anne, who stood off to the side, straight and tight-mouthed, rejecting possible invitations to dance by her "Don't you dare. I'll turn you down, you simp" manner. She might be critical of me in the beautiful low-cut dress, wearing a hair ribbon, dancing ineptly and heartily. What the hell. I didn't, for once, care what anyone might say, and grinned as I bounced past her.

When I stepped into the Bergsons' house the summer I was fourteen and a half, I had no sense of the fascinating, often puzzling world I was entering, a new world full of corners to peer into, to observe and to learn. The job had presented itself as rather ordinary: responsibility for the children when their mother went shopping or visiting, taking care of them when both parents went off on their own. The children were three-year-old Eric and six-year-old Nancy. Laura, the mother, looked like a sorrowing cherub, her smile infrequent and small (maybe she didn't want to show the gap between her front teeth, I thought). She wore no makeup except pale powder and her hair was coiled in rolls rather like those of nineteenth-century English ladies I had seen in pictures. The style suited her, it suited the old-fashioned, many-buttoned dresses on her small, round body, suited her subdued voice and old-fashioned manners, her sobriety and lack of humor; suited because I liked her and chose to hold her unusual, distinctive. It was from her that I learned a sort of child-rearing I had not known before: to persuade with respect in a calm, reasonable voice, to be truly, gently patient. Her concentration on the children's physical welfare and their behavior was so serious and constant that there was little tendency or even time for play. I supplied the games, the nursery rhymes, the stories, and the nonsense songs like "Old MacDonald Had a Farm," which I enjoyed along with them. They had books but few toys and were expected to entertain themselves with a pot, a few clothespins, bits of cloth, empty cereal boxes, to invent games with whatever was around. Getting into the spirit of things, I devised an outdoor game we called "music stones," exploring the myriad sounds that were to be found in clacking different types and sizes of backyard stones together. Laura approved of the musical game and applauded my imagination.

Intelligently malleable, in the main, with each new situation presented by a child, the mother was utterly rigid in a few respects: like it or not, the children had to drink almost a pint of hot water heavily laced with lemon juice and brown sugar (never, never white) each morning. This was meant to help them move their bowels, and well-trained from infancy they did, shortly after finishing the morning elixir. When cause and expected effect did not properly meet, there was considerable consternation, especially on my part when I was alone with the children, as disturbed by the anomalous event as if the whole world had become unhinged. Not entirely a health nut, not entirely not, Laura fed her children the locally baked whole-grain bread, and honey, a "natural product"—the key words —rather than jam. Instead of the classic bologna sandwich for lunch, theirs were filled with avocado mashed with lemon juice. (Lemon, much used, appeared to have a mystic power; yellow like the sun, it might share the sun's life-giving force.) They yearned but never asked for the slice of salami or hot dog they saw in other children's hands. I was tempted to buy some for them when their parents were away, but I was afraid, too bur-dened by their mother's principles and sure that one bite of the forbidden food would poison their cosseted baby-pink intes-tines. However, the same envy with which they watched a boy chomping on a limp gray slice of liverwurst marked the faces of the children who watched Nancy and Eric sitting on their back porch tearing at lamb chops. These were the children of the nuts-roots-fruits-and-berriers, who were allowed nothing but those basics and were, some of them, desperate little outlaws, ripping a bit of cheese or a lollipop from another child's hand; a sudden wail as often as not signaled the rape of coveted food. The desperadoes, after reports to their parents, were reproved and punished both for theft and for breaking the health rules. But the determined (and very hungry) ones became cannier and bolder, capable of snatching packets of candy and sliced ham and boxes of cookies from grocery shelves and fleetly disap-pearing into tall meadow grasses or up trees, chattering like thieving monkeys.

Laura's rigidities about her children's food and drink were stern but rational, as was her conduct generally—except when ominous clouds streaked the sky and winds roared and tore through the trees, promising the thunder and lightning which terrified her. She called the children indoors, tamping down all fear and urgency in her voice. Having settled them with books on the floor in the middle of the room, she quickly took the many hairpins out of her rolls of hair and put them on an outer windowsill of the toilet. It was fascinating to watch the ritual—a particularly primitive ritual it seemed after she told me, out of earshot of the children, that she would surely be killed by lightning if she did not rid herself of the metal hairpins. The children liked to stroke her loosened long hair and never questioned its appearance during storms, and as far as I know, because of the iron discipline that covered her terror with false calm, they were never disturbed by the sights and sounds of weather.

Her husband, Dr. Ivan Bergson, was a dermatologist—the specialty he chose to free himself of house calls and shrieks for help at inconvenient times—and one of the most puzzling people I had yet met; trying to make the pieces fall into an understandable portrait was one difficult course in that summer's dense curriculum. I advanced, in time, to the point where I realized that there were people made of diverse pieces that shouldn't hang together but did; that a lover of the arts was not necessarily a lover of the truth; that elegance abutted on brutality; that my foursquare judgments and evaluations of people had to be loosened, a major push toward maturity. Ivan was slight and exquisite, his enameled smoothness enhanced by shining baldness and shining swells of forehead, like an Oriental ivory figurine. He had a delicate, perfectly bowed mouth that echoed the slight bow-curve of his thin, high-arched nose. Always distinctively dressed, he it was who gave me the golden Borsalino hat and the still dashing old dark-gray raincoat which became the basic components of a costume that, for a couple of years, made the distinctive, unique "I." He had, or had invented, an aristocratic European background, replete with "von" relatives, a faint "Continental" accent that slipped when he was angry, forgetting that he was connected to a "Statspalais" (as he called it) in Vienna; like all young aristocratic bloods, he had seduced bevies of chambermaids before he was twelve. He was the first anti-Semitic Jew I had yet encountered, denying anything but a distant, dim stain in the blood and speaking of some of his neighbors as kikes.

The superior baronial manner and looks were, in my eye and mind, fortified by a large library of books in several languages (something I had never seen in a house before) and a collection of contemporary paintings, much of it gathered in lieu of payments from artist patients. He was baronial as a father and husband as well. A harsh voice emerged from the sleek head to thunder at his timid little daughter—long afraid of him, to judge from her cowering stance when he was around. "If you spill a drop of milk out of that bottle"—a full, heavy glass quart bottle—"I'll kill you." Pale, trembling, her thin little arms taut and twisted, she almost always spilled some milk, once smashing the whole bottle as it slipped from her nervous fingers. She hid from him in the toilet for hours. I wondered why Laura rarely sprang to her rescue. I once ran to help the child, furious with this shade of my own merciless father, and was thrown back with "Mind your own goddamned business."

By the end of the summer I understood why Laura did not rescue her child from Ivan's cruelty. She was, as thoroughly as none of the tough immigrant women I knew had been, his creature. It was for him that she devised the exceptional coiffure and it was to his design that she had her evening dresses made—Renaissance confections of satins and velvets, one Elizabethan gown of panels of pale-blue velvet over white satin, bordered with gold paillettes. (We were of about the same size, and when she let me try on one or two of the dresses and I became rare and beautiful, I could understand her Patient Griselda attachment to a man who could be so brutish with his child and also devise such loveliness.) She had puce silks that looked like great dark rosebuds, and hand-embroidered lawns and linens for winging through lyrical summer nights. To adorn the gowns he bought her delicate, ornate ornaments from a dealer in Chinatown. An exquisite storybook couple, they went to recitals by a young dancer called Martha Graham and to openings at the gallery of Alfred Stieglitz, and were the dinner guests of artists who were filling state capitals and county courthouses with murals. They entertained friends who brought messages

from Raymond Duncan in Paris, from Mary Wigman in Berlin.
Eating with the children in the kitchen of their long, old-fashioned Village apartment I heard from the adjoining dining
room names like O'Keeffe, Varese, Picabia, Bodenheim, James
Joyce. (They had, of course, a pirated copy of *Ulysses,* which I
lifted off their shelves and still own.) This was the style of life
designed for me, I was sure. I would wear dresses like Laura's
and dash around in the stupendous Peruvian llama poncho
owned by the wife of one of the painters; I would talk art and
books, dance and music, and serve exquisite dishes. Meanwhile
I eavesdropped keenly from the kitchen to hear gossip from
Rome, Paris, London, laced with exalted names I carefully
memorized to make part of my discourses. (Of my several sets of
parents, real, fancied, adopted, the Bergsons had, I think, the
most telling effect.)

For the glamour, the clothing, and the jewelry, Laura paid in
heavy coin. It was understood that she try to disregard—certainly not complain about—Ivan's extracurricular flings, which
he, in turn, preferred not to keep too secret; there was no joy in
being a closet Don Juan. A piece of jewelry he purportedly took
back to his dealer for repairs smiled brightly from the neck of a
friend's wife at a Christmas party both Bergsons attended. And
there were several such etceteras of which she told me when we
had known each other for some years and I had become a
member of the household, old enough to understand the patterns of their lives and keep my silence.

One set of demands he made on her came to me slowly. He
would give her long looks after the children went to bed and
waft winsome looks and smiles at her—a vicious little boy—
with hints of "If you'll do it, I promise you something nice."
Sometimes she giggled and nodded a little, sometimes she
looked irritated, frowning as she whispered "No." I began to
know that she had consented, after repeated importunities, to
some sort of sexual variant when he presented her ceremoniously, the Earl of Essex addressing Queen Elizabeth, with a
jeweled mask, small and exquisite ("Maybe a Cellini, who

knows?" he said) or a seed-pearl collar hung with Indian enamels. Or he would announce that next weekend she was to come to town and they would go to the theater, eat in her favorite restaurant, and shop for furs for a new coat.

It was during these absences of both Bergsons, sometimes longer than a weekend, that I felt aged, bent with burdens. First there was the momentous matter of bowel movements. Nancy, in all matters an obedient child, gave me no trouble. Eric sat readily, smilingly, on his pot and for fifteen minutes, a half hour, an hour, refused to perform. He was not angry with me for keeping him on the pot; he beamed and sang a long recital of tuneless songs. I, certain that all the hot lemon drink he had swallowed would explode his intestines if he didn't rid himself of it, was in twisting anguish. I couldn't let him sit, his behind growing redder and redder as it pressed the pot rim, indefinitely, though he didn't complain. I took him off after a long while and continued to watch him closely, waiting for catastrophe. And so it went one time from day to day, for four days, he singing on the pot for an hour and more each day, I shriveling in terror; if anything happened to either of these children I would have to kill myself. After the interminable time, the Bergsons returned, Eric ran to his mother, embraced her, then rushed to his potty and quickly relieved himself of four days' meals and quarts of hot lemonade, the present for his mother which he would not give me. As he emerged from the bathroom he gave me a sweet, villainous smile and asked me to button his pants, which he usually managed without help. The need to strangle him was tempered by admiration of his control, his poise, and the three-year-old wisdom that devised such clever weapons. He became increasingly interesting, this potbellied miniature Machiavelli who knew how to manipulate almost any situation, a knowledge that kept him confident and charming, ready for anything. When he was a bit older, no more than five, I overheard him teaching his sister how to handle Daddy, who terrified her but never him: "Don't let him see you're afraid; try to make believe you're not afraid and he won't bother you. He likes to see you cry, don't let him"—infant wisdom to which I bowed in respect. He was a lot better armored at five than I at fifteen or, I later thought, at twenty-five. Having had a brother who lived in the sun while I lived in the shade, he always young, fleet, and shining, I dun and slow, I could feel with Nancy and tried to show her favor. Helping her with her reading, inventing number games to make her quicker at adding, teaching her to play one-finger tunes on a neighbor's piano, did to a degree diminish the polite, silent distance from me and, slowly, painfully, from the world around her.

Eric and his father had their worlds by a string their women never found. Nancy stayed nervous, retiring, and although she could be lovely and appealing, often covered her heart-shaped face with a hangdog, defeated look. Forced by her father and the irritating ease of her brother, she would sometimes become spiky and brash, frightening herself as a screaming baby is often frightened by its own noise. She then quickly retreated to her usual scared shyness and mute passivity. Her mother, unlike the child, had certain unassailable strengths—the sexual adroitness her husband apparently prized, for one, and her extraordinary skill as a cook. It was one of Ivan's pleasures to search for ancient recipe books (he was a lightweight classicist and medievalist, from whom I picked up greedily names like Phidias and Herodotus, Thomas Aquinas and Grosseteste). From his old books he would pick out a recipe or two and demand that Laura present him with the accomplished dish. I watched her one day with pleased awe as she prepared the feast served a fourteenth-century Archbishop of York on his visit to Durham Cathedral. For one course she stuffed a deboned half-roasted duck with nuts, raisins, currants, ginger, and other spices and herbs, doused with Madeira wine. She then stuffed this duck into another, slightly larger, also painstakingly deboned, then duck within duck was put in the oven, watched carefully, and later served as slices of mixed nectars. The performance and the taste (a slice was put aside for me in the kitchen) were intoxicating to a girl brought up on barley soup, *klops*, and chicken boiled down

to shreds, as they were to the *feinschmecker* friends—all male—
for whom Laura prepared the high ecclesiasts' spread of which
the ducks were the centerpiece. Like Mrs. Roth, like Mrs. Ro-
berti, Mrs. Rosenstein, Fannie Herman, and all the other immigrant women I knew as a child, Laura did not sit at the table
but picked bits off the almost-empty platters in the kitchen. (It
was always shocking to see this "advanced" woman in the antique role of slave servitor.)

One of the men never invited to the connoisseur dinners—
men who wore gray vests and Vandyke beards, showy watch
chains attached to heirloom watches, one sporting a monocle
which he never seemed to use—was a favorite cousin who was a
caricature of Ivan, the elegant face and tight lean body reduced
to a yellow-pink melt. They were occasional partners—as I
learned as I lay in bed next to the kitchen, where they talked
late into the night—in womanizing, comparing notes on women
they both had known and conjecturing about a few they hoped
to know better. One dawn I was awakened by their voices close
over my head. It was the cousins peering down on my breast—
my loose nightgown had slipped—admiring, in their words, the
pretty pink skin in its light shine of sweat, the youthful freshness
of the nipple, which the cousin was about to touch when I sat up
and stared at them. I wasn't afraid of the cousin, whom my
mother would have called a *graubyon* or a *ballegullah,* both expressions for coarse, foul-tongued, and dirty-minded men. I
could have dismissed him with "What the hell do you think
you're doing? Get away from me, you fool." Ivan was another
matter. Why, with his fine tastes and affairs with worldly
women, salivate over an adolescent breast? (I was still naively
trying to put disparate pieces together.) I was also afraid that
any protest from me would produce an angry shout, as he
shouted at Nancy, and I would be paralyzed, as she was, as I was
when my father had shouted at me, as I was—and still am—
whenever I heard a loud male voice spraying anger. If Ivan was
sufficiently annoyed with me he could, over Laura's ineffectual
murmured protests, fire me and I would have to go home, to

stay there as little as possible, to wander for hours if I couldn't find a friend at home or sit in a library growing hungrier and hungrier because I would have no money and was stubbornly reluctant to take food from my father's kitchen. So I said nothing, Ivan said nothing, and pulling the sheet well over me, I turned toward the wall. The cousin smirked at me through breakfast, but no one said anything and I soon discarded the incident, no new experience in a progression of encounters that are now headlined as child molestation and are as old as the earth.

I enjoyed the job when I was in town, enjoyed the children and even the effort to infuse life and ease into Nancy, but found it more difficult when I was left all alone in the country with a three-year-old and a six-year-old. Intensely a city child, I was afraid of the country dark and its inexplicable sights and sounds: the scratching of a field mouse, the swoop of a bat outside the window, the scramble of a raccoon on the roof. Like most of the local houses, the Bergsons' was a plain, loosely built bungalow of wood, a house vulnerable to rain and winds, and I often considered Laura's pale, mute hairpin rituals justified when lightning cut the sky and thunder shook the small house. As in most of the bungalows, the kitchen was centered around a kerosene stove, ours distinguished by erratic habits. One night, when the children were in bed and I was frying a couple of eggs for my supper, the flames from the burner suddenly shot up, attached themselves to the butter in the pan, and, strengthened by the extra fuel, soared. I couldn't reach the screw to turn the fire off; it, too, was lapped by the wild blue flags of flame. As I watched the flames shoot up to lick and tease the wood of the ceiling (there was no canopy over the stove), I became knots of nausea and pain. "Don't panic, don't panic, don't panic," I repeated, because I knew no prayers. When the flames actually began to eat the wood I would waken the children and get them out of the house. There was no phone, no fire department to alert, no one within earshot to yell to for help. I could save the kids, but before I walked them to the nearest neighbor, the house might burn down. I would be responsible for the immense loss and how would I pay for it? I would have to commit suicide, the solution for any huge guilty burden. "That's for later. For now stay calm, don't panic, watch the flames." (The control I soon managed must have stemmed from early admonitions to take care of my crippled little brother, to watch and comfort him at times and in places in which I felt as lost and frightened as he but was already trained at five not to betray anything but calm capability. He was not to cry; see, I wasn't crying; I would take care of him.) And suddenly, as the flames danced before me, I was sitting on the street tending my baby sister in her carriage, cut by a whiplash of shock and horror in finding that the carriage was overturned because I had been reading and let it tip over. She was not hurt or even surprised, but I never recovered. Here, again, I had not taken care of them, an accusing voice shouted at me. It never occurred to me to blame the Bergsons for keeping such a faulty, dangerous stove, for putting *me* in immediate danger. The fault was mine because I was there, because I must have done something wrong. My fault. My fault. Always my fault, as cripples were my fault and beggars and cross-eyed people.

The flames did not chew up the roof boards, but slowly ebbed and died. I did not have to awaken the children, but I kept staring at the kerosene burners after I had turned them off, suspecting anthropomorphic malevolence—the sneaky nastiness of inanimate objects. Contenting myself with cheese and bread for supper, I dumped the kerosene-soaked eggs down the toilet and leaped back immediately into mea culpa—maybe the fatty mess would clog the toilet. My God, more trouble. I had heard of girls leaving houses and children who were too troublesome, but I could not resign, not only because it meant a return to the Bronx, to be delayed at all costs, but because I had learned that there was no backing away from difficulties and had become almost arrogantly proud of my endurance, and control.

From month to month, my life became almost inextricably

bound up with that of the family, in the country and the city, relied on to take care of the children at any time, under any circumstances. In spite of Eric's attempts to poison my life with his empty potty, I found him enchanting (as my little brother had been at three), shrewd and ready to give advice—anything from how to feed a cat to making a folded paper hat, an unctuous Uriah Heep smile, as he spoke, on his rococo putto face —yet baby enough to sit stark naked on the street before the city apartment, waiting for Birthday, a benevolent friend who was to arrive imminently, carrying a sack of toys. I learned him better when we were quarantined, he with measles, while his mother took care of Nancy, who had scarlet fever. We were in widely separated sections of the many-roomed apartment and in contact with each other only as voices through doors and the swift handing in and out of food trays. Laura would not go near Eric and kept her distance from me when we accidentally met in the hallway. When Eric turned restlessly I was afraid, and afraid of his hot, blotched face. I had no knowledge of fever except as a dreamy long time in bed when I was a child. But I learned to put cold compresses on his hot forehead—his mother did not believe in medication for children (or possibly reliable remedies did not yet exist). Carefully following her instructions from the notes she slipped under our door, I became as involved in his symptoms and as anxious as a young mother, coaxing him to eat, loving him greatly when his fever ebbed and he became coherent again. Troubled by the fear that he might retain scars if he scratched his measles, probably confusing it with smallpox, I devised finger games, taught him to play "Church and Steeple" and to walk his fingers on me as the "Teeny, Weeny Spider." I sang endless songs, to which he beat time on the bedrail—spirituals, Irving Berlin songs, Russian folk songs with impromptu mock-Russian lyrics, and songs from the endless store given me by P.S. 58—"Funiculi, Funicula," "The Minstrel Boy," "Jingle Bells," "Drink to Me Only with Thine Eyes," "Believe Me, if All Those Endearing Young Charms." When he had learned most of these, I resorted to the blues and what were then called "race" songs, as sung by Ethel Waters, which I just about understood and he not at all, though he was mesmerized by the slow, sinuous rhythms and the rough, salacious voice with which I sang them. (It might have amused him in later life to know that his musical life began with "Get off, get off your knees, Papa. Turn in, turn in all your keys, Papa. You can't get me back that way," and with the "Handy man who churns my butter and strokes my fiddle," songs I learned from records owned by the "fast set" in the summer community.) Eric and I also pushed the long days away by drawing pictures and tracing letters, which he had begun to learn by himself, sounding out "Cold" and "Hot" on the bathtub spigots and transferring those sounds to other words. We traced his hands and mine and pasted paper stars and suns and animal shapes on the wall, on his headboard, wherever his short arm could reach.

Through the passing days I became more sure of his needs and responses, of his affection for and dependence on me and my affection for and dependence on him. It was living with Eric alone and constantly that created another dream image of a future me. I saw myself vividly, and felt comfortable, as a mother of twelve children, a large, benign, patient earth mother who looked like Aline MacMahon; a mother who never flashed her hand at a kid, who never said "Scratch your ass on a broken bottle," never said "Bang your head against the wall" to a bored child; my children would never be bored. This dream of myself in yet another ideal role shaded but did not erase the me that would be Joan of Arc, Shaw's Candida, Portia, ugly, courageous George Eliot. (They were full-costume portraits, with more to come of personae to try on, to keep testing for their attractiveness and suitability, all but the perfect *one* to be discarded at some wonderful, revealing time. I did not know then the adult character in a Sartre play who says that "every morning I put on the me that matches my coat"—suggesting that the adolescent collection is never entirely closed but keeps seeping thoughts, gestures, words.)

A different sort of mothering, not as satisfying as being Eric's mother-vassal, came to me when the Bergsons went abroad for a month after the children were well, and the employment office in school called me to fill a temporary job that required an experienced baby-sitter—really a teachers' helper, they assured me—in a boarding school that was part of a castle in Washington Heights once owned by the sculptor George Grey Barnard. It was a very long trolley ride from James Monroe High School in the East Bronx to the rustications and crenellations that housed the school which viewed the Hudson. I enjoyed the ride, learning new neighborhoods, new streetcars, new houses, new kinds of dress and faces. Sometimes I walked the distance, as I frequently did from school to home, taking pleasure in my swinging legs and arms and the fine machinery of my lungs and heart.

The school, whose name I cannot remember, was owned and conducted on the principles of leaving the children almost entirely unbridled, an educational tenet popular among advanced groups like those of my summer community. I had often wondered about the "freedom" of the Bergson children. Certainly Laura allowed her children greater freedom than the shouters and smackers and "Where were you?" mothers of my childhood street. But her children were bound in other ways: they had no street life to bang and roar through, no stickball and fights over who held the ropes in Double Dutch, no cabals of plotting, no breathtaking, bizarre sexual revelations, no alignments in fealty or enmity, no politics; in other words, no society of their own, without adult interference.

The castle children had their group societies but were, in addition, permitted to shriek "No" to food, to baths, to going to bed, to lending or returning a toy. "No" was the battle cry of the castle, and it was my role to relieve the regular teachers of the most exhausting nursery group, abundant babblers and wetters, to ease them into quiet for supper and sleep, actually the toughest job of the day. I was ready for them thanks to

Laura and a few instincts I had grown on her soil: how to hold a
child who was by his own shrieks and sobs being tossed into a
wild jungle of hysterics from which he didn't know how to
emerge; how to divert a "No" by a smile, a joke, a pat; how to
speak in a whisper so that a curious child, interested in the
words and manner of the new teacher, would stop his yammer-
ing. After working in the castle of the tall, dim rooms most
afternoons and evenings for several weeks, I was asked to stay
on—not as a substitute, but a regular assistant teacher. My prior
loyalties were, however, to the Bergsons, already returned to
New York, from whom I could continue to learn of the ways
and riches of the world, about what Stein and Honegger were
writing and Soutine painting, about Eugene O'Neill and Susan
Glaspell and the Provincetown Players, about the experimental
Habima Theater; to hear haunting, incomprehensible poetry,
to conquer bits of their world, which would become my landscape, my native climate. In any case, I had missed their
children.

Slowly and sporadically I had begun to sense other people's
feelings, growing up to sympathy, and some of the castle
school's children had an extraordinary effect on me, a girl who
had felt until recently only her own discomforts and pains. One
wide-eyed hyperactive eight-year-old boy, still a bed wetter, a
ceaseless masturbator, a stammerer, and omnivorously eager to
be patted, embraced, or merely touched by anyone, was the son
of a showy free-love couple. The parents had been legitimately
married for a few months but now loved freely wherever they
lit. The mother was made up and dressed to resemble the legendary vamp Theda Bara, wearing massive rings and heavy
ropes of multicolored beads, the effect reduced by bony wrists
and ankles and a flat chest. An actress of now and then small
parts and a maker of lame little poems, she comported herself
with the petulant allure of a star. Papa was a writer, rather
popular in a limited and pallidly radical way. He was disheveled,
dirty, and given to long lectures—into the air, to a captive
audience of children who stood politely still and bewildered for

a few minutes, then slid stealthily away—on the subject of poetry, on the joys of drink and revolution, on the ecstasies of sex,
a wonderful astonishment to me, who had never met a writer or
a parent who wandered so loudly in such forbidden forests. Nor
had I ever met a parent who was drunk, as he seemed frequently
to be, though I knew little of the comportment of drunks other
than the wobble and drag of Mary Sugar Bum, who used to
warble and beg on Lafontaine Avenue. Both parents came on
most visiting Sundays, she with her coterie, he with his, taking
care to meet now and then for the exchange of a couple of
cliché insults that slammed at her sluttishness, his drunken
filthiness.

She greeted her boy, when he ran wildly at her, with a light
kiss and a pat on the shoulder, asked him if he'd been a good
boy, and left him, to stroll the grounds like an artiste at a society
rotogravure lawn party. The father tried harder, too hard. He
insisted on joining baseball games with the other fathers but was
so unsteady on his feet and so dangerously inept that another
man had to take the bat from him. Little Sitwell, named for a
literary crush of the father, began to howl, outraged. Because
his father was not allowed to play? Because he was so shamefully
drunk? We tried to explain to the child that the sun in his
daddy's eyes made him dizzy and he couldn't see the ball to hit
it; lots of people had trouble with batting when the sun was in
their eyes. The child's mother made no attempt to comfort him
and we didn't urge it, keeping him away from her anticipated
mutterings of "That stupid, shitten drunk." My childhood had
been replete with domestic quarrels, in my house, in houses that
blasted their furies through courtyard windows, but I had never
heard a parent shamed in this way before his children; our
parents' fights were mano a mano, shouting mouth to roaring
mouth, no snide mutterings.

Broken little Sitwell hurt me and I was hurt by six-year-old
Franny, who played peaceably near the other little girls—washing toy cups, dressing and undressing dolls, smearing the paper
on her easel with water paints—all done quietly, slowly, while

she wept. She never made a sound, no sob, no pull of breath, simply a ceaseless well of tears out of an unnamed sorrow. The most moving adult was one of the "old" teachers. "Old" to an adolescent might be forty, and that was probably the age of the very plain woman with coarse hair and potato features, an intelligent, dignified woman who had—the gossip went—approached a man of her acquaintance and asked him to impregnate her; she desperately wanted a child. Whether she didn't know the hazards of a late first pregnancy or would not succumb to the information, she carried the pregnancy to term and produced a boy with marked symptoms of Down's syndrome, a sweet, docile child, open-mouthed and oblique-eyed, who could learn almost nothing. His mother spent interminable hours with him on her lap, after her classes were over, trying to help him count on his fingers, to say his name clearly, to say hers, with little success. Watching her and living intimately with Sitwell and the tiny blond Niobe became insupportable. I was pleased to leave the school and its pain, although life there with its vamps, drunken poets, and curious variety of other aberrant parents was, in its troubling way, a revealing journey into the widening world for which I was insatiably greedy.

I returned to my role as assistant mother at the Bergsons', where the climate was less charged but as highly colored: the new book, the new picture, the swooping capes, the flaming hennaed hair, the bushy beards, the paint-stained overalls, the African jewelry, a vat of bathtub gin in the kitchen, women stomping in batwing fancies, shrieking like banshees, and no next-door neighbors to complain because they were also stomping and shrieking.

During my second summer with the Bergsons, when I was fifteen, I had met Martha, probably at one of the entertainments so frequently and ardently staged by the community. I became enmeshed in her. She was Diana, the lithe Diana of the hunt, her movements like the graceful sway of tall reeds; her fingers were long and she joined them in circles and arcs as she spoke, the compelling punctuation of an East Indian dancer. We were the perfect pair, I thought, she dark and vertical, I fair, short, horizontal. She must have been aware of the striking contrast we made, because she wasn't averse—I yearned for it—to walking very close to me, her arm around my shoulder, my arm around her waist. We caught a good number of glances, a few amused, a few censorious because we were being showy in this place that pretended to have no pretenses, because maybe we were attempting to appear to be lesbians, a fashionable stance among those teen-age girls who were avid to read Radclyffe Hall's *Well of Loneliness* (difficult to obtain), of which we heard and spoke a good deal. And there were the titillating shadows on Virginia Woolf and Vita Sackville-West, etched a little too subtly in *Orlando*. And what about Willa Cather and what about the poet H.D.? It was a distinguished company, and a number of intellectually ambitious girls, not prepared to join it, liked to feel linked to its members by dress and gesture, no more.

Martha and I didn't see each other as often as I liked and I never surely knew how important it was for her to see me. We hid potentially emotional words in smart, light commentaries on the stupid world and its stupid people. It was easier to be with and worship her when the summer was over and I could cut classes to meet her downtown at her school and ride the subway with her to her house. I eagerly performed errands for her: a music book in one of the secondhand music stores then on West Fifty-seventh Street or downtown on Fourth Avenue, where I might also pick up a copy of the *Oresteia*, for a classics project in which she was to read Electra. I was willing to do anything for her; the long subway rides to search out music and books were holy ventures, as a devout young soldier might march in the Crusades, as the palace slave Charmion might serve Cleopatra.

Although she invited me to her house, I rarely went, preferring to meet her away from the angry glare in her mother's onyx eyes. As she slowly took in my long, worn mouse-gray coat, my black stocking and black sneakers, the golden man's hat, she

stripped me of all charm, character, intelligence, of my very
being. Behind the tight lips, behind the thick eyebrows and the
hair harshly pulled back as if she were trying to tear it off her
skull, I could guess the thought that moved through the minds
of several mothers I knew: "Dresses like a crazy, not like a girl,
not even like a boy; practically homeless, no ties to anyone,
obedient to no one. So she works, she says, in a laundry and a
library and takes care of a doctor's children. I wouldn't let her
touch my children. And she's spoiling my Martha, interfering
with her practicing, teaching her to answer me back." I never
heard her rebuke but knew this sort of rapaciously possessive
parent of a talented child who would carry the family into riches
and glory—shades of my father. To fulfill her mother's fantasy
Martha must succumb to the unceasing vigilance of the harsh
eyes under the aggressive eyebrows and to orders from the
sharply defined, almost metallically edged lips. Priding myself
on being a rebel, my raison d'être of the time, and working the
role for all it was worth, I had expected attention, possibly
admiration, or at least acceptance, from a family of avowed
Marxists, who should approve of the freedom I had wrested
from capitalist convention. Faulty logic or great innocence.
Mrs. Alpert's politics had nothing to do with the fact that
Martha belonged, all of her, every breath, every cell, every
thought and word, to her mother and to her ambitions for her
daughter's success in the capitalist world. Her attitude toward
her husband was even more chilling than her disdainful manner
toward me. I could escape but not the brown man who looked
like a pumpernickel loaf and was as simple. He adored his
daughter and liked to make little jokes with her, into which Mrs.
A. cut with a phrase of contempt: "Stop already with your idiot
jokes." Or worse still, called Martha away from her father into
the kitchen on one pretext or another, leaving him foolishly
suspended in midsentence. I liked him and was sorry for him; I
had never seen such a steady attempt to annihilate a person
totally. When my mother and father fought they gave each
other full size and sound, equal, well-matched adversaries.

The only other member of the household was a young cousin who was registered at City College from the Alpert address although his parents lived in New Jersey. He seemed to come and go at will, without comment from his aunt; she had no ambitions for him. His attitude toward me, the few times we met, was familiar: an awkward nod and a dash for the door after we were introduced, a few muttered words on the second meeting, a third meeting during which the fear of appearing friendly bred nastiness. He told me that I looked like a horse when I made my nostrils flare. He had me; it was one of a number of affectations I tried on during those years—the flaring nostrils meant sensitivity. I dropped the flaring nostrils, which must truly have looked grotesque, flapping and waving like fish gills, and took on other mannerisms that attracted me and were, in turn, discarded when they became a source of embarrassment. I pitched my voice very low and kept forcing it lower, for dramatic effect, until I was addressed on the telephone as "Mister." Simultaneously with the dramatic contralto voice, I devised a manner of walking in a slow, stately stride (as stately as five feet two inches would allow), with my eyes fixed poetically on a far horizon. The seer's stride and vision once knocked me hard against an unyielding subway turnstile, and the blow to my stomach pushed a loud, pained grunt out of my spiritual, otherworld face. I was wrapped in hot shame, as if a large, critical crowd saw the blow and heard the brutish grunt, although the station was actually almost empty. It is difficult to know when the putting on and taking off of affectations altogether stopped, certainly not until later and not until I became easy and trustful with one or two people whom I loved and who seemed to love me.

The censor of my nostrils left for another college. Life and love with Martha dwindled to a halt through a progression of causes. Her mother had learned that we had slept together in their country house while she was in the city. Although we lay stiffly holding hands and carefully not touching each other's bodies, Mrs. A. forbade Martha to have anything to do with me.

Martha wasn't completely obedient, but she had been invited to work with an amateur chamber group who were more experienced and older than she, and felt the need for more practice; her mother's admonitions not to spend time with an undisciplined sloven folded smoothly into Martha's ambition. I continued, however, to meet her at her school and ride the subway with her. There seemed to be less and less to talk about; she was becoming increasingly laconic and I too discouraged to continue babbling on my own, sensing the futility of being constantly bright and arresting.

When I went early the following summer to live with the Bergsons, I found that Martha had acquired an attractive new friend. She was very blond, delicate, curly, and, compared to my dun shabbiness, dazzlingly chic. She had a cute, feminine name—Bettina, or something like that—and apparently had a clothing allowance that permitted her to wear several striking costumes: from flirtatious headband and hair bow down to her shoes, she was all in one color—a yellow set, a green set, a lavender set, with bag and handkerchief to match. She talked quickly and smiled a good deal and flirted with man, woman, child, dog, cat, and, of course, herself. I was envious and jealous, furious with Martha for taking this froth of bubbles as a serious friend, of paying so much attention to her breezy burbling and, worse, admiring her meticulously matched wardrobe. Bettina refused to notice my presence and never spoke to me, closing a ring around Martha and herself, locking me out. That Martha consented to my being excluded was a terrible blow, not, though, as deadly as I had thought it would be were we ever to be separated. Shocked, bitterly displeased, and yet a little amused, I watched Martha and pert Bettina walk as Martha and I had, an arm embracing a shoulder, an arm embracing a waist, and decided that the effect was posed and fakey, Bettina, so blond and curly, hanging on the straight, flat length of Martha like a parasite vine.

I tried to make Martha's indifference, her heartless perfidy, a dagger to my heart and venom in my veins. Her cruelty was the black swift path to a noose or a leap off a high roof, to the suicide I had promised myself if she ever left me. She *was* leaving me, and I found (though acknowledged reluctantly since it contradicted the view of myself as boundlessly faithful, in spite of love's wounds, to the death) the fact acceptable. What sustenance would Martha get from Bettina? She didn't know Dostoevski from Elsie Dinsmore, nor César Franck from Irving Berlin, but was endlessly informative about where to have yellow shoes dyed pink. And what about Mama, who would certainly not permit the child of her plain-thinking, low-living house to listen long to such decadent frivolity and its little threats; maybe soon even boyfriends. I was—it took some time to admit—growing tired of them, the pumpernickel father who smiled as no one smiled back, the forbidding mother, whom I later recognized as the twin sister of the famous Grant Wood woman, and Martha herself, turning to me, when we met by chance, her mother's disapproving face. There was no farewell speech, no dramatic act of parting, as I had envisioned it, my eloquent, accusing monologue battering at Martha's shamefaced silence. We faded from each other like objects in a fog. I heard considerably later that Cutie had taken her rainbow wardrobe to a boarding school and that Mrs. Alpert and Martha had moved to Philadelphia, possibly to be close to the Curtis Institute, and probably leaving behind—almost absentmindedly—the unimportant father.

The Bergson children inevitably grew more self-sufficient. Since I was no longer needed as mother's summer help, the children now capable of bicycling and running around on their own, I looked for other summer jobs, the most memorable one in a loft on the Lower East Side, where fifteen or twenty girls of my midteen age pasted "diamonds" into junk jewelry. It was easy and monotonous and earned five dollars a week. We were probably illegal child labor, without protections, with little air and no fans in the hot loft, but we were pleased to be working and earning. At first I was captivated by the shape of the stones, whose unpolished tails were cut as shallow cones. A small cupped stick dipped in glue picked the gem up by its face and the tail was embedded into the cone-shaped hollow in the metal. We had to be careful that the jewels were well planted, using a pushing twist, that there was enough glue, but not too much, on the stick. When I learned there was a bonus of a few cents on ornaments filled beyond the daily quota, I stopped being entertained by the cones, the holes, and the sticks and worked fast, trying to earn money that would buy me total freedom—an importunate need for some years—from my father's house and earnings. (I seem early to have realized how vengeful independence—from some fathers, some lovers, some husbands—could be.)

The job had other satisfactions. It was near Joe's place of work, and it was a glorious thing to show off a cavalier, not good-looking and with a slight accent, and yet a man friend who waited night after night for me. Once in a rare while Mark came along, sad enough to excite the other girls with his air of intense, doomed love, like Ramon Novarro. From the loft we wandered through the East Side streets and into a line of shops that made long-tubed Russian cigarettes, which I smoked as I had seen it done in a movie, held between the tips of thumb and third finger, the hand cupped under the cigarette. Practicing the exotic gesture on the streets—streets of *sheitels,* of young girls in long black stockings and long-sleeved dresses, streets of the Orthodox, of yarmulkes and prayer shawls—I was halted by the broad body and blazing eyes of a bearded, black-hatted man, as wide and firm as a wall. He called me a *kurveh* (whore) and cursed me in Yiddish with black years and cholera. Then he spat on the ground before me, wetting my shoes. He frightened me, not as my father had, with punishments here and now, but as a supernatural force who would hate and doom me forever. He was the messenger of a Jewish God who would drown the world, the messenger of a furious Jewish prophet who, I once read, howled imprecations at the "Daughters of Zion with their stretched-forth necks and eager eyes." Bold and immodest, I

took it to mean, and un-Jewish, as I was being. There had been
times when I squirmed away from my parents' accents as they
revealed them to strangers on the El or in Crotona Park, and
times when I was pleased with my mother's pert "Polish" nose
and the fact that I had *goy* coloring, blue eyes and blond hair,
and the small nose as well. In spite of these passing breezes of
anti-Semitism and having been raised in a nonreligious house,
neither Yiddishist or Zionist (my father was more fervid about
the union movement than about the striving of Jews to return to
some distant Arab desert hole), I could not think of myself as
anything but Jewish, if it meant only loving Jewish songs, very
funny, very sad. The spitting old Jeremiah threatened a firm-
ness, a spine, a strong support that I didn't want shaken; I might
briefly, tacitly, deny Jewishness, but it mustn't deny me. (Encounters with groups of black-clad, bearded men striding pur-
posefully through the Orthodox streets of Jerusalem are still a
threat, still capable of spitting, cursing and denying me for my
unsheiteled, unshawled head, my lipstick, my cigarette, abomi-
nations all.)

Occasionally I would visit with Laura Bergson as with a friend,
sitting in the kitchen with her, talking about school and jobs
while I watched her prepare an interpretation of a menu once
ordered by Tiberius, or maybe Napoleon, and to be served to
Ivan and several special guests, a writer on food and wines
among them. Why had I not learned to cook from Laura, nor
even remembered clearly any of her dishes other than the
duck-stuffed duck? My mother's contempt for all matters domestic except child care had seeped into me and left a stubborn
stain. Her worse than mediocre cooking, I sometimes suggested
to her, was a form of revenge on my father. No, she said,
laughing, it was a nice idea, but it didn't work; he was accustomed from childhood and the years he was a boarder in
America to just the kind of food she made. And we certainly
had become big and fat on the repetitions of stuff she cooked.
And what about the potato latkes and blintzes, a lot of trouble,

of which we couldn't get enough, and the fried matzo we consumed in great mounds during Passover? "In your own house
you'll cook more fancy, more Yankee." As for cleaning, polish-
ing, neatening, straightening, and all the other domestic busy-
nesses which, I once complained, she didn't teach me as other
mothers did their daughters (obviously a plea for intimate
mothering that I unexpectedly wanted), her answer was dismis-
sively curt: "Any girl who isn't an idiot can learn everything
there is to keeping a house clean and neat in a half hour. All it
requires is that you must want to do it. If you want to show off to
your neighbors and relatives what a *baleboosteh* you are, you do it
a lot. I'd rather go to school or work. So it isn't so shining neat
here. For who? Your father, who doesn't notice anything except
where is his paper? For you? You and your brother make the
disorder and I'm not going to run after you both all the time,
straightening, cleaning up. If you want your books and pencils
neatly kept, keep them that way. It's your business, not mine."
She was right; when the time came I found the skills of house-
keeping quite simple, arranging the time and will to do it much
more difficult. I learned to cook fairly well eventually, never in
Laura's class but, like Laura's, acts of slavish devotion. When
devotion seeped away, with it seeped the willing passion for
ornate, painstaking cuisine. A trustworthy, objective barometer
of my love life was the plunge from Grand Marnier soufflés
under the most effulgent of suns to burned hamburgers for the
storms and shipwrecks.

When the Bergson children went off to college and their parents moved to the country, I saw them rarely, and they gradually left my life except as vibrant memories and gratitude for all,
in myriad ways, that I had learned from them. It might have
happened in any case, without them, but I prize them as the first
spurs and witnesses of my growing up. They trusted me with
their children, their houses and the money and jewelry they
contained, their paintings, their records, and their books, of
which I stole, as mentioned, only one. They were not critical of

me or my appearance, rather abetted its singularity with their esoteric Villagey hand-me-downs; they accepted me as the adolescent I was, with a mature sense of responsibility but otherwise a bright kid shouting into all the corners of the earth for answers to her own ill-shaped, garbled questions, searching for an "I" into whose shape she could nestle comfortably, a form that didn't pinch or prick. Laura, especially, understood the rattling handful of mosaic bits called Kate and was certain, as I was not, that they would sometime join each other smoothly. Noblest of all Bergson virtues was that they never said or even suggested that I was a *meshugge*, a word thrown frequently at me at home.

4. HARLEM, ETC.

A new friend, May, was my number two Carola Polanski (the daughter of our janitors on Lafontaine Avenue and the first and only professional prostitute I've known). May was not as good-looking but a lot smarter, fixing a schedule with a couple of traveling salesmen rather than playing the broader, more hazardous field. Her school attendance was about like mine, full of holes, though she didn't spend her truant time in the library; she curled her hair and polished her nails and slept and shopped. Nor did she shop in Klein's on Union Square as we did, and that rarely. Her clothing looked like the ads of the big stores in the Sunday papers and she had reached the supreme acme of her own place, a one-room kitchenette apartment in Manhattan. Other than a double bed, a small table, and a couple of chairs, it had little furniture and the icebox was almost empty, but this was *living* and I felt honored each time I visited. One Friday evening she asked me if I'd like to go to Harlem; she had a date with some friends there and we'd have a good time. As usual inwardly leaping forward with eager curiosity and at the same time cowering back in fear, I said coolly, "Sure." She, dressed in her low-necked purple satin, squeezed me into a black silk dress with long, tight sleeves. "Black makes you look skinnier and older." After a long subway ride from her place on

West Sixteenth Street, we reached Lenox Avenue and made our way among clusters of houses and people I had never known before. They were, for one, several shades of brown, talking, laughing, and dragging at bottles on the stoops of their houses. Their clothing was frilly and brilliant and their children slender sprites who nudged and teased and ran restlessly among them. At one corner, we stopped at a stall lit with kerosene lamps and the shine of fatty meats with a rich hot smell. We had pork sandwiches—particularly delicious because so defiantly nonkosher— and some conversation at the stall and walked on the short distance to the dance hall where May was to meet her friends.

It was a large, low-ceilinged room, dimly lit except where the band sat at one side, under bright lights that glistened on the saxophones and the oiled hair of the drummers. On the opposite side, a series of small lights over the faint gleam of glasses on a bar. (Prohibition concealed the bottles.) On the dimmed dance floor shadowy figures twirled, dipped, kicked, turned, made grotesque shapes as in a dark etching of a witches' sabbath I had seen in an old book. May and I were greeted by a couple of Negro girls. Her chumminess with them, a foreign breed to me, was awesome, as if she had easily floated across a great abyss; my friend May was a citizen of several worlds and I was very proud of her, flattered to be in her company. The girls pointed across the floor and we snaked among the dancing couples until we came to a tall, middle-aged light Negro man walking toward us and, immediately behind him, a younger, darker man. Introductions were made. May began to dance with the younger man and I was taken onto the floor by the older one, a sturdy man with a round, pleasing face. I knew how to dance, somewhat, but usually refused to because I thought I was too fat and felt ugly and was always aware of my feet as Chaplinesque—my father's description. Almost, I could lindy hop, but I had seen it described as "riotous" and as "a flying dance done by couples in which girls are thrown away." I couldn't stand the idea of being thrown, flung like a large, heavy sack, so much manipulated; I resisted, square and stolid. (I often think that fifteen overweight pounds changed the course of my life. For one thing, the sheltering in intellectual pursuits might have come later and less avidly if I could have lindy hopped really sensationally, and I might have known less serious and more playful boys, with whom I might have spent more playful, foolish hours.)

I told the man I didn't know how to dance. With, "I'll teach you, honey," the man put his arm tightly around my waist and I was skimming the floor, turning, bending, swinging, acquiescent to the skillful suggestions of his arm and fingers. He seemed pleased with himself and me and kept me on the floor for another dance and yet another. During the third dance his guiding arm grew tighter, his other arm joined it at my waist, and he began to grind his belly against mine. As I tried to pull away, the arms held tighter. He smiled down at me. "You're a nice piece. A friend of May's? How come I haven't seen you here before?" Still trying to pull away, as politely as I could, I said that I had never been there before. "Well, I'm glad you finally came. How old are you, honey?" I gave him my stock answer, usually acceptable. "Seventeen." He laughed. "The time of the sweetest, juiciest peaches." Still holding me tight against him, he began to lead me to the edge of the floor, toward a dim area near the bar. He then backed me up against the darkest wall. His hand with the big onyx ring began to rub my breasts while the other arm held me tight to him, his erect penis pounding at my belly. I couldn't run, scream, or try to hit him. Nor did I want to. I had gotten myself into this, maybe actually wanted to, and should have known what to expect. I struggled timidly, but couldn't act offended or angry; it was all my fault. Still clasping, rubbing, pounding, he said huskily, "Let's get out of here. I've got a nice place down the next block and we can come back to dance later." "No, I'm sorry, I have to get home, my father'll kill me if I don't get back soon." "Aw, come on. It's too late to worry about your father." He looked at me, studying my face for a moment or two. "You're scared, aren't you? I'll bet you're a virgin. We'll fix that; no use carrying around a thing you don't need. That cherry's going to be busted one of these days by somebody, why not me?" I didn't know what to say or do, I didn't know how to escape, and if I did were the subway trains running? Where was the station? I was bound in panic, doomed forever, lost to whoredom and disease, as my father had promised. The man, feeling my terror, released me and led me to the bar, where he bought me a bottle of soda which I tried to drink. My strangled throat couldn't swallow it. He stared at me for a long while. "You're no May. You're no seventeen. White girls who come to Harlem come for one thing, black prick—supposed to be bigger than the white thing—to buy or to sell to, and everybody knows it. You're not ready and I hope you'll never be. Come on, let's get your coat now and I'll walk you to the station." As we left the dance hall, he grasped my arm firmly, angrily. "If I ever see you in Harlem again I'll whip the shit out of you, much worse than your father would. I mean it. You know I mean it."

At the station he paid my fare, told me where to change and to stand in the middle of the platform, where I could yell for help to the man in the change booth if anyone bothered me. There was no one else on the platform and no one came except a rat, out of one hole, a nervous shrewd look around, and into another hole. The subways were not then dangerous places, but I was afraid, afraid of the rat, of the station, of the black tunnels on either side of it, of the silence, afraid of my lack of courage, afraid of May's contempt if she would ever bother to see me again. After an endless time, the welcome rumble and the roaring light and I leaped into the nearest door, to sit near a sleeping black woman in a ragged coat held together by safety pins, a shapeless knit hat slipping to her eyes. She roused herself at 149th Street and stumbled out with me, to slant to a bench, asleep as she fell to it. I left her there, bereft of the comfort of her sloping presence, and waited for the East Side train whose slow progress would take me through familiar stations—Freeman Street, Simpson Street, Intervale Avenue—stations that were the addresses of my schoolmates, friendly stations that allayed fear; home, if I would admit it. When I got off at Allerton Avenue, the clock on the candy store window near the station accused me with two-thirty; the street lamp glared balefully. It was an innocent, peaceable neighborhood and there was little reason for fear, but I had acted like a bum, a whore, and I must be assaulted and raped, fulfilling my father's prophecy. As I ran, my own footsteps were those of a pursuer, someone who would tear me apart.

Relieved by the sound—as soft as I could make it—of the key in our apartment lock and the door shutting behind me, I stood trying to calm my breath in the dark entrance hallway; ebbing panic gave way to resentment over our peculiar sleeping arrangements. The bedroom that might have been mine and my sister's had been given over to my cousin Bessie, for the duration of one of her long separations from her husband; my father's niece of the weak bladder was especially appreciative of the room's proximity to the bathroom. This left a convertible couch in the living room for my young sister to use, and either my brother or myself with her, depending on who arrived earlier. (Its eccentric machinery suffered when my brother, now a large, well-fleshed adolescent, disturbed its balance as he got in. The couch began to fold slowly of itself, rolling both occupants toward the center and threatening to crush them like insects in a Venus's-flytrap. My resigned sister would wearily call "Sandwich!" and both would pull themselves out to push the sides down again.) The person to arrive home last had to take a cot out of the hall coat closet, extending its folds, dropping its feet quietly to the floor, and reaching high on the closet shelf for blankets and pillows, careful not to pull down a shower of clattering hangers and their coats. I could have pushed my way into my cousin's bed. Unthinkable. With the determination to keep late hours which my brother, a lover of sleep, hadn't yet achieved, I had learned to set up the cot smoothly, without much noise.

It was doubtful that I had awakened them; they must have been awake for some time, to judge from the intensity of the whispering that came from my parents' bedroom, off the hall-way. As I lay on the cot, fully dressed, I could hear his voice: "Where does she go? With whom does she run around so late at night? You don't know? Why don't you know? Are you her mother or not? Who but an idiot, a criminal, lets a girl so young run around in the black hours? You're making a prostitute of your own daughter."

"No, I'm not. Maybe you like the idea, you talk about it so much, you've been talking about it since she was ten, even younger. Another father would worry about an accident, maybe, but you always find your way to the same idea—street girl, whore. I know she isn't and won't be and she's a lot older than fifteen. Do you know any other girl who since thirteen has earned her own lunches and carfares and even clothing, a girl who stays on through high school in spite of a father always putting rocks in her way? How long is it that she's taken money from you or me? She's even stopped eating here because you keep talking about how much butter costs and chopped meat, while you feed the fat, ignorant sisters you brought to America. And maybe soon another niece, and who needs her and the expense she'll be. And why is Bessie in the bed that should be your daughters'? She's fighting you and has the right to. She has a right to a father who encourages her, who helps her. Why do strangers, teachers in school, praise her, push her on, while you try to break her legs? She won't let you, she's becoming a *mensch* in spite of you. Leave her alone!"

"Leave her alone? Leave her alone wherever she likes, with whoever she likes? No-goods, street people, dirty people, dis-eased people, drinkers, maybe gangsters even?"

She broke in on his customary litany of horrors. "Stop it, already. She's foolish, all kids are, but she isn't a fool. Shut up and go to sleep." But he was wound up, driven, and couldn't stop, repeating and repeating, his voice growing louder, his words stronger, more urgent. I could easily picture his distorted face and flailing arms and suddenly imagined that he was about to hit my mother. I jumped off the cot and yelled, "Shut up, you in there. If anybody was going to make me a bum, it would have been your shitty nephew Yankel. Ask him what he tried to do to me. Ask your pal Mr. Silverberg, who took me to the movies to feel me up." I was about to mention Bessie, who had had her kind of fun with me when I was younger, but she was standing at her bedroom door, staring. (And anyhow, my bed experiences with her had been more curious than menacing.) I shouted, "Ask your friend the one-hand-under-the-sheet barber, Tony, who gave us all such cheap haircuts. And it could be that you knew about them all." As I felt again the anguished turns under Tony's pinstriped barber sheet, the twisting under Yankel's thrusting body and onion breath, the imprisonment by Bessie's grabbing thighs, the crawling of Mr. Silverberg's fat spider hands, my fear and shame in Harlem that night, I burst into an explosion of weeping. Sobbing, bellowing, "I always thought you knew it all, and didn't stop them, didn't try to protect me." I pulled my coat on, kicked the cot over, and started out the door. My mother, tight-faced and pale now standing in the hallway, asked where I was going. I didn't know, but I was never coming back. I would let her know when I had a place. She said nothing, she didn't ask me to stay, she didn't cry. When we were out of the apartment, near the stairway, she thrust five dollars into my hand, saying, "Take care of yourself." No embrace, no kiss. We didn't do such things, and in any case I needed to stay untouched, firm, gathered on myself. As I walked down the stairs, Mark opened his door, dressed in his bathrobe. He had of course heard my shouting and weeping, and repeated his offer to find me a room and pay for it; he could be dressed in a moment and we could find a room together. I hated him, too, and his wounded dark-eyed Russian love, another burden to cope with. I told him it was too early in the morning to look, for the time being I would stay with a friend, and dashed down the stairs.

There was no friend. After I had so profoundly disgraced her in Harlem, I couldn't go to May, who was probably not at home yet and wouldn't be for a while. Minnie's mother, who said I was

a bad influence on her daughter—I lived like an unbridled
shikse—certainly wouldn't let me in at four in the morning and I
really didn't want to see or talk to anyone. I walked and walked
swiftly in the damp morning, winds swirling leaves off the trees
as I wanted dank, ugly things to swirl off me. I strode through
the gray dawn and rainy morning, clutching my five dollars in
my hand, my coat open to the healing cool dampness, from the
upper Bronx to the big library at Forty-second Street, my safest
haven. The library was not yet open when I got there. I sat on
the stairs watching thousands of people rushing to work, some
of them quite young. Almost as young as I? Could I learn what
they did, filing and stenography and good typing? Could I lie
about my age and sell things in a store? Maybe I could get a
full-time job at the laundry near school for a while? That is, until
I got a job as a chambermaid on a ship to Europe and then
hitchhiked slowly through France and Italy and Spain. Or until
I went to a far-off college and worked my way through as part-
time librarian among thousands of books in ivy-covered buildings on wide, long greens. Lulled by these dreams, I went into
the library as soon as the doors opened, to wrap myself in noble
words, to weave a soft cocoon of words around my life and
being, to make smooth the lumpy, irritated, confused thing I
was.

Reluctant to break the five-dollar bill tucked deep in my coat
pocket, I had no lunch but did feed well that night for fifty cents
at Childs near Grand Central. White-tiled and unadorned, like a
public rest room, the restaurant suggested the women's waiting
room in the station as a place to sleep. I had seen, in the several
times I passed through, many sleeping women looking forever
glued to the benches. After strolling along Madison Avenue
and Lexington and glancing into the local hotels (a quick look; I
didn't dare go in), I entered Grand Central Station and, hesitating, made slowly for the women's rest section. There they
were, the women I would rather die than ever be: the cracked
shoes, the swollen, splotched naked legs, the frayed, stained
sweaters, the matted hair held by one comb or a twisted rag. I

thought I could sit with them, at least through the night (or until the police threw us out) but it was the open eyes that weren't seeing, the ears that didn't seem to hear, the haggard faces without expressions, that soon drove me out of the station and to circling the emptying nearby streets.

Where to get some sleep on four dollars and change? I knew nothing about the Y's and their accommodations. The only possibility that presented itself was to tempt Minnie's mother with my four dollars. She was no poorer than the rest of us but had a passion for hats, and I might tempt her with the price of a new hat for two nights of sharing Minnie's bed. She and Minnie were about ready for bed when I rang the bell of their apartment on Fox Street. Mama opened the door with "What are you doing here this late? My husband's in bed already and we're going to sleep in a few minutes." She didn't shut the door on me, though. Very quickly, bold with fear of defeat, I said, "I had a fight with my father and I'm afraid to go home. Would you let me sleep here for two nights? You don't have to feed me and I'll pay you two dollars a night." I took the four dollar bills out of my pocket and offered them to her. She muttered some sort of assent and took the money. Minnie gave me her towel so that I could wash up. Face and hands clean, my underwear dingy with a couple of days' wear and wanderings, I slipped into Minnie's bed, hugging the outer edge. I had no right to crowd her, particularly since I was going to lie to her, make up a story of a beating by my father because I came home late from a party. Since I had to lie to her, she was not that night an intimate friend, and I kept my careful distance as I told my quite ordinary story.

Without books or notebooks, I went off to school with Minnie, who had put an extra slice of buttered bread into her brown paper lunch bag for me. School registered only dimly. What did it matter that I hadn't read the chapter on the Civil War for my history class? I couldn't describe the fission of amebae in the biology class and I wasn't embarrassed. It was all far away and unimportant. There were two dimes and two nickels in my pocket. There was no choice of action but to go home at three o'clock, long before my father would be there, to see my mother, to whom I could admit defeat, with difficulty. She greeted me with a surprised smile. She didn't ask me where I'd been, what I had done, where I had slept. She suggested I could use a bath and a change of clothing and, if I was hungry, there were some fresh rolls in a bag on the kitchen table and farmer cheese in the icebox. After I had bathed, dressed, and eaten, we sat down together, looking at each other. After a long while, I said, "I don't want to live here anymore, but I don't know where to go." "I know," she answered, and added, "I have an idea you might like. What about the Goldens? They're nice people, and with all those relatives coming and going, they must have lots of room and beds. Maybe you could teach little Clara the piano—and sit with her. If that won't cover your rent, I'll give them a few extra dollars a month; they won't ask much."

Mrs. Golden and Clara were at home and both enthusiastic. Clara wanted a big sister to share her room, Mrs. Golden liked any new, interesting situation, any change, and she sparkled at both of us out of her Tartar-slanted ice-blue eyes. Mr. Golden, she said, would have no objection; we knew how good-natured he was and how much he thought of me. As for the money, don't worry about it. We're doing all right, thank God. That evening I moved my books and clothing into Clara's big closet and was launched, on Mr. Golden's courtly welcome, into the merry, talkative family, of which I soon fancied myself a member. Memory exaggerates, but I hear constant laughter as I think of them, laughter when they were arguing politics, laughter when they ridiculed distant relatives (of which there seemed to be thousands), laughter when the overcooked spaghetti became a wad of paste. It seemed as if laughter lived of itself as a member of the household, and ruled it during the almost incessant playing and partying. There was a gaggle of young people —whose nephews, cousins, and nieces they were I never found out—who traveled almost constantly. With each arrival and departure, bottles of homemade wine, steaming heaps of stew and noodles, bowls of fruit compote, cakes stuffed with raisins and nuts, dishes of chocolate kisses and nonpareils. Relatives came from Brooklyn and from New Jersey and even from other sections of the "coops." I was always invited and maintained a balance of "Of course, thank you" and "No, thank you, I have a date," careful not to overuse their kindness. The happiest part of the parties was the dancing that followed the feasting. It was unstylish, laced with a touch of horas and Russian kazatskes and polka hops, everyone dancing, even grandma. The couple I found most engaging—and educational—were a slender cousin and his fat young wife, a pretty tub of happy pink cheeks, ripe moist lips, and a full, broad, round bottom. They had their own immutable style: she clasped her arms around his neck while he kept his hands outspread, covering as much of the juicy flesh as he could, on her bottom. It was fun to watch as a frank, mutual expression of sexuality which I had never seen before—and would not again until I began to frequent French movies.

All good things must end, and too soon, I had learned. The summer was coming on and the Goldens were going to spend the vacation months with their ebullient tribe in a big communal farmhouse. Everything in me—my blood, my breath, my uncertainties and hungers—urged, begged, "Take me with you, please. Don't leave me." But of course one never said such things, never betrayed such weakness. We all embraced, promised to see each other soon, and that was that, except for "Where am I to live?"

5. THE WOMEN

It may have been talk among my teachers in the music and English departments, it may have been my artistic "Lower Depths" costume, it may have been an expression of her own needs, but an English teacher, Marian Wood, with whom I had no classes, engaged me in conversation in the lunchroom one day. She continued to seek me out in the lunchroom and in the halls, to arrange that I walk to the subway station with her after school or, if I wasn't working, to have a cup of hot chocolate with her in a local coffee shop. It grew and grew, the relationship she fostered so vigorously and which I didn't understand. She had learned that I was running the risk of being expelled from school, that I was exploring perilous courses like Harlem dance halls (I couldn't resist broadcasting my adventure, with some fancy edging to embroider it); she could assume that I was poised for all sorts of flights into enlightenments and trouble. (She was one of a numerous breed of teachers in her time whose efforts went beyond teaching: efforts of involvement, of persuasion, and, if need be, rescue, generously and often astutely achieved and I may have appeared, in the beginning, simply a subject for such help.)

One Friday afternoon she asked if I'd like to go to a matinee on Saturday, if I was not working. I dashed to my laundry and

begged to be allowed to work two extra evenings the next week
instead of Saturday afternoon. The boss was good-natured
about my hours, possibly because I was such a dumb bargain as a
worker, and I met Marian at the theater she had mentioned.
This was the opening of a remarkable series of events which I
don't think I ever completely understood. I was a bright girl, a
raw girl, a well-read girl, a self-destructive girl, who it was hard
to imagine merited all the attention, time, and money she lav-
ished on me. We went to frequent Saturday matinees or to
afternoon concerts (to Marian I owe, among many other debts,
Lotte Lehmann and the German lied) and then on to dinner at a
large, amiable Italian restaurant favored, she told me, by lib-
erals and intellectuals. After dinner, another theater performance. I never paid for anything but my subway fare. It was a
glittering world and I danced through it with joy, with delight
at being chosen as a companion to an educated adult, a teacher
at that, still a word as exalted in my lexicon (though I would
never admit it) as it was in my mother's. No one ever had valued
me with such steady enthusiasm. And always, in the pleasure,
the nagging little "why?" Why me with the Luna Park mouth
and the "blond-nigger" hair, according to my father's description? "Why" slowly faded when I began to visit her house on
Sundays, with increasing frequency. Although she did most of
the talking, she was careful to ask me my opinion of the play we
had seen the night before and of the chicken cooked Tuscan
style we had eaten. In the main, she taught in her own lively,
nonstop fashion. She told me about places in Paris where she
had lived for a while, she told me about Socialist friends in
Berlin and the bitter, political drawings, banned in the United
States, of George Grosz, about *New Masses* magazine and its
cartoons by Art Young, about anarchist friends in London, and
in each city she sketched the shade of a lover. Women with
lovers were supposed to look like Camille or Nefertiti, while
Marian was slight, with the full, round face and the bright, alert
eyes of a squirrel. Yet I never doubted a word she said or

listened for false tones under the words, as I did with other adults.

A new note soon crept into Sunday conversations, these mainly with her crony Helen, who seemed always to be there. Marian would point to me as if I were inanimate, a statue, a puppet, and say to Helen, "Look at that gesture! And that long neck and the subtle smile! She will be a fine lover someday." I had no notion of what she was talking about—a lover for whom? And with my fat thighs and ugly big mouth? Whatever she meant, it came peculiarly from a small squirrel lady, a schoolteacher who wore navy skirts and oxfords. Was she being sexy—and to what purpose—as well as maternal, as well as my best teacher? But I refused to worry long about the odd words and observations, preferring to remain the choice protégée of a royal household which had so much to give me. I actually saw the forbidden George Grosz drawings, in a folder she had smuggled from Germany. She showed me European artbooks I had never seen, by artists I had never heard of: Bonnard, who painted with brushfuls of sun; Braque, thoughtful and honest; the sinuous, delicate menace of Japanese courtesans; the Coney Island blare and the despairing streets of artists she called the Ashcan School. Art was not enough; there were music and books in her rather frantic rush of force-feeding culture. From her large record collection she picked out *Fidelio*, too much for me, too heavy, too hortatory. I wasn't ready for Beethoven's opera and she cleverly went back to Chopin mazurkas, her recordings carrying little gems only vaguely related to the battered shreds of sound I had heard from too many tenement windows. Marian gave me books to read: de Maupassant stories, the poetry of Heinrich Heine in a German-English edition, a bilingual copy of Baudelaire's *Flowers of Evil*. Though deeply impressed with the hot, tangled phrases, the perfumed odor of decadence, the *"luxe, calme et volupté,"* I could no more cope with these *Flowers* than with *Fidelio*. Eager to appear capable of understanding anything that was written, since Marian seemed to expect it of me, I went to the library for a book about French poetry and quoted, as my own, in my own vocabulary, the judgments of Baudelaire I had picked up. Marian was impressed with my critical acumen, turning to Helen with "Just listen to that, will you?" I didn't like lying to her, but lying to adults was still not too difficult. I absolved myself by buying a recording of Debussy's "*Après-midi d'un faune*" for her. The gift moved her, as an offering out of my meager earnings and as a reflection of the advanced musical taste toward which she was speeding me. (I see myself, over much time and distance, as a project, a piece of work toward a degree of prime importance which had to be achieved rapidly. Or was she, like my father, wrapping a fantasy about me, a dream daughter who would make *her* life glow, enacting a most subtle form of child abuse?)

When summer arrived and with it the departure of the merry Goldens, Marian put several English Department heads together and a summer camp job emerged, as assistant to the dramatics counselor and supervisor of a group of fifteen- and sixteen-year-old girls, one or two of them older than I, who had as usual represented myself as older, eighteen. It was a difficult summer, much tougher than my summers with the Bergsons, a time of trying to cope with campers' adolescent cruelties and furies, of desperate improvisations on the design and execution of costumes, about which I knew nothing but had to seem knowing. I didn't think much of the broad green horizontals and dense green verticals of what might have been a pleasant landscape; the landscapes that spoke to me were city streets. Never having been to a summer camp, never having known anyone who had, I found it essential to learn quickly the vocabulary and to use it in recounting fraudulent former camp experiences to my bunkees. There wasn't much else to learn from them, actually, besides the routines of games, crafts hours, and meals, and to appear authoritative, even commanding, to girls older, richer, and—I had to think in self-protection—dopier than I. The sour grapes that made acid scorn of their white shorts bought at Best's, the skirts from Lord & Taylor's, the fluffy angora sweaters and exquisitely boxed cookies from B. Altman's, were one weapon of self-protection, another my superior vocabulary and overprecise, careful speech.

None of it has stayed with me, not one girl, not one counselor, not the name of the camp; nothing, no one except my boss, the drama counselor. She had informed me as we sat together on the train going to the camp that I was to be responsible for the costumes for two big parents' day productions, *Alice in Wonderland* and *Peter Pan,* and they had to be showy, impressive proofs of the camp's creativity, among its other excellences. Unless I wanted her advice or criticism, the designs for all the costumes were to be my creations, and for putting them together there was somewhere in the camp a sewing machine, and a lot of varied materials in the storehouse. I had doodled costumes in my history notebook and had watched my mother use a sewing machine but had never tried it, encouraged by my mother to avoid the skills that, she felt, had imprisoned her. The only sewing I had ever done was the fine hand stitching that went into the awkward, slightly musty graduation dresses we made in the last grade of elementary school. Insisting, after several troubled days, that I couldn't find the sewing machine, that it must have been discarded, I began to sew all the costumes by hand, working through the nights on the challenges I had set for myself. The *pièce* of *Alice in Wonderland* was a close-fitting coattailed suit made entirely of black patent leather for the Mad Hatter. The costume for the dog in *Peter Pan* was made of pieces of rough rope, unraveled into hairy matting, then painstakingly pasted and sewn to a pair of pajamas. The costumes elicited fervid admiration from parents and my bunk charges, who showed surprising pride in their counselor's achievements. I was called out of the props tent to take a bow after the creditable performance. After she had taken her second bow, the drama counselor joined me in the props tent, spoke her gratitude and admiration, and unexpectedly enfolded me, murmuring endearments and kissing my eyes and hands. I was too tired, too relieved that it was all over, to be much impressed; maybe she was acting out of relief and exhaustion too.

Amy was a tall, slender woman with close-cropped shining brown hair, who wore boys' shirts open at the throat and trousers—not then common among women. She was both graceful and awkward, as a young boy often is, sometimes mute with shyness, at times lyrically voluble. After the costumes and props were put away and the parents left, dropping souvenirs of money and candy as they departed, we both had more time, time for me to walk with her on a tree-lined path outside the camp and to row with her on a nearby lake. She liked to point out slivers of moon and the stars nesting in their curve, she asked me to admire the changing silhouettes of the trees as we glided by and the diamond sparkle of drops as they fell from her raised oars. She spoke of her friends, poets and actresses and painters. It was a delicate courtship, no more kissing, no more words of endearment, simply lyricism as it glowed and sparkled around us and unrevealing bits of biography, tentatively offered.

After a few weeks of walks and rides, when we seemed to have grown comfortable with each other—a little formal, but easy —I found her in the washhouse, scrubbing my laundry, left earlier. For a moment I hated her. How dared she? What colossal nerve, to invade my privacy, to be intimate with my socks, with my shirts, with my bras, my panties! She was trying to close in on me, as Mark had, burdening me with a weight of devotion I couldn't and didn't want to understand, affection that must demand more in return than my limited gratitude, all I could and would give. And maybe now not even gratitude. I hadn't asked, never would, for this bit of slavery, this ugly symbol of devotion, of a grotesque dream marriage. I had heard the girls in my bunk giggling about her and other counselors. They said the women were lesbians, girls' camps were full of them, and they teased me for being the pet of the most conspicuous of the local lot. They were an uneducated but shrewd bunch, frequently justified in their rude judgments, but I was not going to be instructed or intimidated by them. And then there was my insatiable curiosity to be fed. So in spite of the invasion of my laundry and the threat of cloying devotion, I continued on the walks and lake rides, sometimes winsomely, flirtatiously trailing my hand in the water like the lissome girls in English films who spent their blond youth punting on the Cam. The hand stopped trailing the waters prettily, the curiosity waned, the discomfort swelled, when Amy began to recite love poetry and described in greater detail, with more glowing praise, the friends she would like me to meet and whom she was sure I would love. She was slipping more and more of Mark's ropes around me, trying to pull me closer and closer. I knew I would be forced to free myself, forced by a too exigent gesture she must soon make.

The night it happened was a soft night with a pale moon, the stars misty. As we walked, Amy put her arm around my shoulder, turned her face toward mine, and kissed me, long and deeply. I pulled away from her as gently as I could. Here again, as in Harlem, I had gone to the edge of a cliff and couldn't blame the cliff. This was my fault; I should have stopped it days and weeks before and chose not to, flattered and curious, wrapped in a light delirium of power. As I tried to find words to discourage but not hurt her, she grabbed my hand and in an urgent voice begged me to come to live with her. We would go anywhere I liked—France, Spain, Italy, Greece, where she would dedicate her life to me, to keeping me happy forever, and I would never have to worry about money or jobs again. Drowning in this flood, I turned quickly in the direction of the camp, walking rapidly as she walked behind me, calling, "Think about it, please think about it seriously. I mean every word I say to you." Had I known then that many sexual approaches carry the words "forever" and "I want to make you happy," eva-nescent clichés, I would have been less impressed but with little experience, I took the phrases in their full, solemn, literal weight, made heavier with the guilt of having evoked them.

To avoid Amy in later days I told the girls to say I was out when she approached the door to our cabin, or hid in another bunk when I thought she might be looking for me. She soon stopped asking for me, but I could see her sitting on the stairs of her cabin looking across to ours, and soon that, too, stopped. In a cruel mess of contempt, guilt, and mockery, I joined the other girls in a teasing game of nude night swimming, posturing, leaping, revealing as much of ourselves as we could, watching to see if Amy was watching us from her cabin near the pool. We all insisted gleefully that we could see her—there, behind the trees, in a corner of the porch, behind a window. We probably never saw her after a first glimpse and her swift recognition of the hurt we were trying to inflict on her; she was a sensitive, dignified woman, who wore away the remaining camp days in as much seclusion as her job would allow.

When I jumped off the train in Grand Central, my summer job over, it was into the great vault of a Byzantine church, the information desk its exquisite chapel. The surrounding sky-scrapers were clustered like majestic, gleaming waterfalls, the slender city sky was alive with forms, with gorges and hills in red brick and shining white stone. The women in their city dresses moved like dancers, the men were as slick and taut as toreros. Over them all—sky, buildings, men, and women—a heat haze, a tremulous, delicate mist that tasted to my skin like honey. This was my habitat and I floated through it in a state of grace. Woolworth's and its enchanting city gimcrackery was my first place of welcome. Having feasted, I took the subway to Marian's apartment and spilled a witty stream of complaint: all the greenery I could accept was about the size of a city block, more was too much; the girls in my bunk were crass and ignorant, when they weren't outright stupid. (Not then, or in letters be-fore, did I mention Amy, except flatly as the dramatics coun-selor for whom I worked. For reasons that weren't clear, I had a feeling that more talk about Amy would open a Pandora's box and I wouldn't know how to handle its evils.) Marian told me about her summer, in a distant corner of Connecticut, and the interesting friends she had made, people I would meet when we

went there for a weekend, soon. Would I like a sandwich before
I went home? No, thanks, and I wasn't going home. For the
time being I would probably stay with Rosie, whose mother was
a grumbler, but a quick forgetter of grievances, and between
her job, no husband to look after—the legend was that he had
run off with a greenhorn boarder some years back—and her
Workmen's Circle meetings, not much at home anyhow. In the
meantime, I would look for a full-time job and transfer to an
evening high school. Marian looked dismayed; so much of her
effort and expectancies to be washed away in drabness, in or-
dinariness. "But you seem to forget," she said, "about the college scholarship my friend is trying to arrange for you. I haven't
talked much about it, but now it looks almost sure. They don't
require math, and your English record, and the very good
chance that you'll get the English medal when you graduate,
should get you a creative writing scholarship, maybe as soon as
next year." As I leaped at her with eagerness for more details
and assurance, she said, "Before we discuss anything else, go to
see your mother, who's been worried about you and it would be
cruel to keep worrying her." (Something I rarely thought of
and will feel dreadful about into my grave.)

The visit home was stiff. My mother didn't ask me why I
hadn't written her all summer, why she had to find out if I was
all right by calling Marian every Saturday morning from the
corner drugstore. When I told her, as I had before, as flatly as I
could, that I was not coming back to live with the family or with
the Goldens, that I was going to work and attend evening school
and find myself a room somewhere, she said she couldn't blame
me for leaving. Only keep in touch and if I needed a few dollars
to let her know; she would send it with my brother if I didn't
want to come to the house. Her pretty mouth was tight in her
white face, her fingers tightly clasped in her lap. I put the things
I had left in a big paper bag, said good-bye, and went to the
door. I would have liked to speak the sudden wild sadness I felt
and, as sudden and profound, the sympathy I felt for her. But I
didn't know how. Hesitating at the door, I said good-bye again.

She didn't move. I walked out, closing the door gently behind me; no abrupt final noise.

Rosie's mother was not especially pleased when I appeared, but she was busy preparing to visit friends and hadn't much time to object. More important, Rosie was the sun in her life and she didn't want to displease her, possibly lose her as my mother was losing me. Instructing us not to burn the chicken when we reheated it, not to leave her our dirty supper dishes, not to track up the kitchen floor; I was to wash my hair, it looked messy, and wash the sink afterward; there was a blanket folded into the cot in the corner of Rosie's room (no sheets, but I was accustomed to that), and Rosie wasn't to forget her Jewish homework for her Shalom Aleichem school, and we weren't to talk all night, she threw a fringed Russian shawl over her skirt and blouse and dashed out. School was not yet in session and Rosie and I spent delicious days visiting with friends. I told highly colored stories of my life in camp (no mention of Amy) and they talked about new boyfriends they had met as mother's helpers in the country, their stories as richly embellished, I suspected, as mine. On the money I had earned during the summer—mainly tips from parents—I treated Rosie to the movies and big ice-cream cones, and to win her mother's favor, supplied the breakfast bagels and farmer cheese. She was impressed; such an adult, nice gesture, maybe I was outgrowing my irresponsible *bummerkeh* stage.

The days with Rosie and her mother exhausted my money. Reluctantly, I decided to visit my laundry to ask for a full-time job; it would be infinitely easier to talk to Vito, the Italian boss who liked to pinch my cheeks and my behind, than to search want ads and stammer my way through interrogations about my age and experience to an inimical business face that I always imagined as lean, hard-jawed, gimlet-eyed, as immobile and unresponsive as a mannequin in a store window. I was also worried about job applications that would ask my religion; "Jewish" might damn me and I refused to lie, bound not at all by religion but by a firm tribal loyalty. The day before I was to see Vito, however, a letter arrived from Marian's place in the country, addressed care of Rosie. She had a job for me that offered room and board, it wouldn't interfere with my part-time jobs nor with continuing at James Monroe High School. One of Marian's friends needed a mother-sitter, someone to stay several afternoons and evenings with her elderly, widowed mother, someone to run errands and keep the old woman company when the daughter went out.

I knew the forbidding, sharp-voiced Miss Sonntag slightly, and had a premonition that I wouldn't please her. She was quite amiable, or at least very polite, as she explained my job and asked if I could start—bring my things—a few days later. There was no bedroom for me, but a convertible couch in the living room, which contained, as well, bookshelves, pictures, and a baby grand piano. The coat closet in the hallway had enough room for my clothing, and a cabinet next to the closet would serve for the rest of my wardrobe and my schoolbooks. A Negro lady came to do general cleaning and the laundry—not mine—once a week. I was to see that the bathroom and kitchen were clean and to do some light dusting between the cleaning woman's visits, said Miss Sonntag. As she spoke, I wanted to like her. I couldn't; her voice was too commanding, she was too large, blocking out all the space and air around her, and her square head reminded me of the people of my unfavorite painter, Léger; her big jaw was like part of a machine. I can't think that she liked me either, but she needed me and it was her social duty, Marian undoubtedly told her, to help a gifted girl who was drawn to the brink of trouble.

It was a proper, respectable, uncomfortable place, everything placed squarely and neatly, the furniture always highly polished, the window shades always at the same level, the white-enameled garbage pail always gleaming in its immutable niche.

The shining white garbage pail, infinitely more refined than the tin bucket kicked around in my mother's kitchen, seemed too fine a container for used sanitary napkins—I had long graduated from strips of old sheets—so I stashed them for a couple of days shortly after my arrival in a paper bag in my cabinet, intending to dump them in a street basket. But I never seemed to find the opportunity to take them out of the hallway quickly and inconspicuously. I hoped the Sonntags wouldn't notice the hideous stench that was growing out of the cabinet and filling the hallway. Reproval came dryly, tersely, from Miss Sonntag: That terrible odor, it was rotting sanitary pads, wasn't it? I was to wrap the soiled pads in the old newspapers under the kitchen sink and put them in the garbage pail, which was placed outside the door for the super to collect every night. Intensely miserable, feeling loathsome and filthy, I wrapped the bag in huge wads of newspaper under her unmoving eyes and jammed it into the pristine pail. The shame hung on my chest like a big rock. I took everything out of the cabinet and scrubbed it. I bathed carefully every night—not my Lafontaine or camp habit—and still the stink was on me for many days.

Miss Sonntag remained correct, stiffly kind, and even persuaded me to play piano duets with her. I was out of practice and resistant, nor was she very skillful, so the results were halts and starts and abused passages, but when we were able to do a page or two properly together it was so satisfying, so happy an experience, that I liked her in spite of her Léger face and voice. Those times I called her Sara, as she had several times asked me to, though I usually had difficulty forcing such intimacy from my mouth.

The mother was small and round, with little features, like my mother, and, like my mother, eager for merriment. She walked with difficulty—I never knew why—and few neighbors visited her; Sara discouraged what she called "tenement sociability." There were no grandchildren for impromptu, after-school visits; her other children and their spouses visited only on weekends, though they spoke with her frequently on the telephone. She read a good deal, she talked long with the once-a-week cleaning woman, learning much about her dour days, but it was still a lonely life and a limited one for such an animated, intelligent old woman. It was at least partially because she was lonely that she greeted me so effusively when I got back from school, and quickly told me what the cleaning lady had recounted that day, the funny joke her youngest son had told her on the phone, and that the super's wife was pregnant again. Then we made a grocery shopping list, the last item always, "Buy yourself some cookies or chocolate or whatever you like." The evenings that Sara was out, Mrs. Sonntag told entertaining stories about her youth and early schooling on the Lower East Side, and remembering, she laughed as my mother laughed, with a flood of tears rushing down her cheeks. Convinced that I was not lovable, was a self-centered slob, I had to admit that she probably loved me, or something close. Although I was confused by the many uses of the word "love" and wasn't at all sure of how it should feel, I almost certainly loved her, the grandmother I never knew, and like the baby brother I once took care of (now embedded in a sturdy pubescent boy), weak in the legs and dependent on me. To keep her entertained during our evening hours together at the kitchen table, I would note and record everything I saw and heard around me: the two bedbugs that crawled out of the library book of a girl who had been boasting to a friend that her mother was an ardent cleaner; the old woman who approached me at a bus stop on a cold night to say, in Yiddish, "Don't be such an *elegantke*, wrap your shawl around your head." (How did the woman know I was being Eleonora Duse, the romantic shawl lifting and dropping picturesquely on my shoulders as I heroically braved the wind?)

I told Mrs. Sonntag about Mr. Goldberg, in whose English class we had spent one whole semester listening to him read *Green Mansions.* He looked, I told her, like a counterman in a delicatessen, round and moist, and he had the expected concomitant Yiddish intonation. That was an exaggeration, but he did have a cantorial lilt, usually controlled, except when he was carried away. And Rima, the heroine, carried him away; he was in love with her as if she were real and his own true palpable love. I liked to imagine fat-nosed Mr. Goldberg imagining himself a slim, blond lover in a loincloth, a poetic Tarzan, caressing the long, shining hair of his beloved. Mr. Goldberg was abetted by a unique accompaniment, almost a musical obbligato, to his reading. One of the girls in the class had riches of red-brown hair, her star attraction, and she pinned it around her head in a variety of inventive styles that required a battery of pins. As Mr. Goldberg's Chassidic cadences trembled in adoration of Rima, the girl slowly removed the hairpins, one by careful one, releasing one long red-brown loop and then another, placing the hairpins in her lap carefully so that not the faintest tinkle might sound. She ran her fingers through the garlands and swags of hair until it was all down, shook her head a little, and then sat enraptured, elbows on the desk, fingers intertwined beneath her chin, half-hidden and mysterious in her silken tent. We all waited for the moment in the reading that would inspire her act; inevitably it came; inevitably we called her CooCoo the Bird Girl, a then-famous freak attraction in Coney Island. Mrs. Sonntag was enamored of Mr. Goldberg, Rima, and CooCoo the Bird Girl, and I reported the events of each class, introducing as many entertaining details as I could invent. I also told my responsive old lady about Mr. Cantaro of the History Department, a short man who looked a bit like Adolphe Menjou and was a passionate admirer of Napoleon, stressing his hero's amours as he looked out the window at the schoolyard, searching for the lost, heroic world that was rightly his and, we generally agreed, to show off his supercilious profile. She also learned from me all of Dr. Huebner's primitive, effective teaching jokes. Her favorite was the story of a soprano soloist singing with an orchestra led by a very animated conductor. Boy in a distant seat: "Why is the man with the stick beating the lady?" "He's not beating her, he's leading the music." "Then why is she screaming so?"

Eavesdropping in the grocery store, on the bus, in the school lunchroom, everywhere, I brought to my old lady vignettes, witticisms, stupidities, weather reports, news of dry stringy bushes losing their last leaves. I complained to her about a movie hero singer who looked and sounded like an empty can, probably affected by my mother's earlier judgment of him as "a blond shitter" (much more contemptible in Yiddish). I remembered for her and described the shapes and corsets and bras I had seen in the crowded communal dressing room of Klein's and the eager-eyed girls who sat on ladders to watch for the thieves who put on one new dress over another and their own old dress over the new obscured acquisitions, then waddled out carrying nothing, paying nothing if they weren't caught. Bringing to my old lady these gifts to color her narrow life was my first experience of prolonged, voluntary solicitude, and a pleasing one. It also made me look at my mother in a new light and imagine her growing old and lonely. I began to visit her more and more frequently when my father was at work, and after slow, formal beginnings—"How are you?" "All right, how are you?"—I began to tell her the stories I told my old lady.

I lost my plump Russian-doll grandmother and my two surrogate mothers, the hot and the cold, within a year. The first move was Sara Sonntag's. Sara liked to keep up with youngsters she had met and encouraged in her years of settlement work, her favorites in my time a group of boys, some in jobs, a couple in college. A few of them were invited on frequent weekend evenings to eat rich cakes and drink big glasses of cream soda and to sing to Sara's accompaniment selections from Franz Lehár and Victor Herbert operettas. Being myself in a pure Bach period, particularly the unaccompanied violin music, which I found dry and undigestible, therefore the acme of great music, I scorned their silly stuff, but as a member of the household—and Sara considered this type of socializing part of my education, too—I was asked to join in and reluctantly did. Between wondering what she saw in them, what they saw in her, didn't they have anything better to do on weekend evenings, and why was Sara's color so high and her speech so excited, I carefully, critically examined them. Tom—a suspect name for a Jewish boy—was tall, with strong features; he sang loudly, talked a lot, moved quickly and flashily, and was very arch with Sara, already the actor he was determined to be. Davy was slight, quick, and funny. I would have liked him more if he weren't obviously enjoying the dopey stuff and if Sara weren't so hectically bright and grotesquely flirtatious when she spoke to him. Danny was quietly polite and clearly there because his friends had dragged him along and he had nothing else to do those evenings. Conversation over the slabs of cake were nostalgic bits that referred back to experiments in amateur theatricals and the fun they all had together. "Remember when Ralph kept tripping on his sword in *The Gondoliers*?" "Remember when Millie forgot the words of 'The Moon and I' and we had to shout them to her from backstage?" I sat and smiled with their laughter, taking time out for several visits with my more entertaining old friend, reading in the bedroom.

The boys' attitude toward me was minimally polite, and vice versa, until Davy began to talk to me, to ask me questions, to say my blue dress looked nice on me. As I stood in the kitchen one evening, filling glasses of soda, he came in with a loud, "Let me help you," and in helping, whispered, "Let's meet next Sunday and maybe take a walk, you and I." He was clearly Sara's property and I suggested, also whispering, that she might be mad. "Let her be," he said, and rattling the full tray of glasses, said, "Three o'clock at the elephant house, Bronx Zoo." Sara was home that day, writing reports, and I was free to meet him. We fell together as if we had been waiting for this for a long time. Since it was late fall and there were few people to see us, we huddled together like the animals and kissed and kissed. In front of the indifferent snakes, before the censorious eyes of the eagles, and the curiosity of the deer and the pacing tigers, we kissed and hugged. On later excursions, because public kissing was rare, we staged farewells at subway stations, at smelly El stations, at bus stops, and expanded our field to Penn Station and Grand Central, where many tracks offered many places for fake leavetakings of high emotion. The very best place was the top of a Fifth Avenue bus, designed for an infinity of kissing and necking on its long route from Washington Square up into Washington Heights. We were soon spending all our spare time together, if only for an hour. The happy, excited dashing and Davy's phone calls should have explained themselves and I decided that lying, a first impulse, would be too complicated and too demeaning. When I announced that I was leaving to meet Davy and would be back at seven o'clock so Sara could get to her concert, the old lady said, "That's nice. Give him my regards." Sara said nothing.

The half-expected complaints began to roll out. Sara had offered me shelter, she said, because she wanted me to be in a steady environment that would make me a good student and possible college material. It appeared to be a wasted effort since I wasn't studying or doing much homework. And I was jeopardizing Davy's record as well; City College made high demands on its students and dropped by the score those who didn't meet its standards. I might consider him and his career, too. How come the top of the piano was so dusty? I had left grease spots on last night's dishes, washed too fast and carelessly, always ready to run. The washcloths in the bathroom were for the face, not scrubbing the basin. She did not, could not, complain about my concern for her mother. Davy and Grandma liked each other, too, and we often spent evenings together, a contented threesome, cracking nuts, peeling tangerines, laughing, when Sara was out. I sent Davy home early those evenings, not so much afraid of Sara's jealousy, but sorry—I was becoming almost human in the refulgent climate of love with Davy, with my old lady, love with myself—for a plain middle-aged woman too much moved by an eighteen-year-old boy, the chosen boy, who preferred a rough-edged, uncouth girl. The smart old mother must have been aware of the unrequited attachment. She was probably sorry for her daughter and impatient of such foolishness, but said nothing about her and rejoiced in us beamishly.

Sara announced one evening that she was bringing in a practical nurse to care for her mother, a woman who would sleep on the convertible couch and would be in attendance all day. There was no obvious deterioration in the mother's condition, but something like this had to happen, this maneuver for getting rid of me. As usual and because I was too happy with Davy to worry, I had no alternate plan. He helped me pack and waited for me outside the house while I said good-bye, now with sadness and open affection, to my old lady, promising to phone her frequently; she was too wise and honest to ask me to visit. Davy took me to his parents' house, a poorer and smaller apartment than our tenement flat on Lafontaine Avenue, crammed with cots for relatives from Williamsburg who carried their own hard-boiled eggs and *challa* because Davy's mother was forgetfully semikosher. And she, direct and fatalistic, said, "What the hell, one more," as she shoved her young daughter to the side of a single bed to make room for me. "You, Davy, sleep where you always sleep, in the bedroom with the other boys, and stay there. No gidgee in this house."

6. "BIRDS DO IT . . ."

School continued and the part-time jobs, including Vito's pinches, and I continued to see Marian on the weekends—theater, concerts, education, restaurants, and all—when Davy had to work or study. Among the techniques of Cubism, the symbolism of Kandinsky, and the novelty of Schönberg's scale were interposed expressions of boredom with my virginity. Again a return to the wonderful lover my neck and shoulders and big mouth promised (flattered always and occasionally appalled as I saw myself as some sort of roast of mouth, neck, and shoulders, followed by rich undefined desserts). Marian knew just the man to lead me into elegant sex after a poetic deflowering.

One spring weekend I met the man, whose first name I never knew; we'll call him Jones. After a mottled career of wandering and working at several trades, he had found himself the leader of a leftist group—several kinds of left, from pity socialism to bombing for anarchy—which settled in a far reach of Connecticut. Largely self-taught, he was remarkably well-read and well-informed, especially in American history, whose most attractive personage was, to him, Brigham Young. On a reduced scale he duplicated Young's life quite successfully. He, too, was chieftain of a small, polygamous tribe, though, as a devotee of free love, he did not take his women in marriage. He had in his wanderings found a Mexican tribe whose design for living he also admired and tried to adapt for himself. The Indians kept one woman, he recounted, for household chores and carrying water from a distant well; another took care of the children, everyone's; one woman was the prime producer of babies; the youngest and prettiest was for love alone. Though it was difficult to find the proper number of women of the proper dispositions for so exquisitely efficient a scheme, he managed well in his narrower pattern. Three of his women were in their forties, career spinsters with enough money to keep a man, at least partially, in exchange for his favors and as pioneers in this unique manifestation of equal rights. One woman paid the rent for his well-equipped, warm cabin. Another kept him in utilities, woodsman's boots, and virile woodsman's shirts. Marian was the best cook, so she provided his lunches and dinners. Preparing breakfast was the ceremony performed by the woman who had "been pleasured," as he put it, the night before. A continuous surprise to me was the fact that the women were polite, even hospitable and kindly, with one another. There was a number four, but she was not of the circle. She was younger, in her early twenties, singularly pretty, it was said, and her cabin a distance outside the settlement. Thus she was rarely seen, but strongly felt, especially since Jones stayed with her for two or three days at a time. It was an impossibly long walk to her house he explained, there was no bus, he had no car or bike, so he had to stay a couple of days. (Clearly, this was the youngster to be used for pleasure in beauty and sex in the Mexican style, I thought, and the others probably thought, though she was rarely mentioned.) Marian explained the various details of their design for living rather proudly, as if it were a privilege to be a member of so singularly advanced a society, a bold step in man's evolution. Wasn't she ever jealous? I asked. Of course not. Jealousy was a primitive thing, an atavism of an urge to possess that was a root of capitalism. How could free, intelligent men and women justify owning each other? I didn't ask again, lost in admiration of these heroic women who could do what I certainly couldn't. I seethed and my stomach churned when a girl tried to link arms with Davy or even touched his shoulder.

A later weekend in Connecticut, a picture-postcard weekend of blossoming trees and blossoms in the grass, Marian invited several local friends, including Jones, for an evening of large, good eating, followed by singing. We sang spirituals and Russian folk songs (the combination a telling symbol of left leanings) to a guitar and a mandolin. Between songs, the mandolin player, a skinny man with a Russian accent and doleful eyes, stroked my arm, brushed pink by the sun, crooning, "Byoochiful, such byoochiful," and asked me to walk with him in the woods the next day, Sunday, to look at "Byoochiful tris end flowvis." Marian quickly took me aside to say that Jones expected to take me to the woods tomorrow for my deflowering ("really *flowering*," she said) ritual. I thanked the Russian, promised him another time, and turned to look longer and harder at Jones. He was good-looking in a history-book-picture way, clear and American, like Thomas Jefferson. He looked almost as old as Jefferson, I thought, certainly much older than my father. But Marian was a connoisseur of lovers, and anyone who pleased as many women as Jones did must be remarkably skillful. I tried to comfort myself with that thought while I worried, still, about the pain my friends told me to expect, a fact that Marian pooh-poohed; a little twinge, a moment's discomfort, a drop of blood maybe, nothing to it—and cured by passion. This technical matter had, of course, nothing to do with Davy though it might provide instruction for both of us.

Sunday was warm and fragrant, and we were given a light lunch by Marian, who thought it would be best for what was to follow. (Her planning offended me, so lacking in poetry, but maybe that was the way of sophisticated, incomprehensible worlds. And then again, almost every situation and person I encountered seemed strange to some degree or other. I had long accepted life as *meshugge,* to use the favorite parental word.) As Jones and I left the house shortly after lunch, I half expected Aunt Pandarus to shout erotic blessings on us, but she just continued to smile from the doorway as we headed across the fields toward a deep stand of birches and flowering shrubs. As we walked, Jones talked of the beauty and fecundity of nature; the millions of blossoms waiting to give way to fruit, their seeds to become more blossoms, more fruit, more seeds. Had I noticed the stuff that looked like spit when we crossed the brook? That was the beginning of frogs, thousands of them. Those nests in the trees before us held new eggs, the birds soon ready to break the shells, then learn to fly and mate, to make more eggs. All these profligate, beautiful cycles were the music with which the male element awakened nature's spirit in the female. In a less exalted mode, I had heard all this in biology class, in another mode in poetry, in yet another in the movies and novels, and in yet another in dirty jokes. He wasn't telling me anything new but was telling it in a rich, measured voice and a cadenced vocabulary—like a ballet to baroque music. At one particularly welcoming and sheltering clump of trees he sat down and gestured for me to sit with him. He continued to speak of the overwhelmingly generous fruitfulness of nature flowing from the mysteries of sexuality, the divine power of sex. A city girl assaulted by the warmth of sun, the odor of leaves and grasses, and breezes of delicate air, I grew sleepy. I tried to keep my eyes wide open, rubbed them awake but couldn't resist leaning against a tree trunk, and fell fast asleep.

An easy explanation, among a couple of others, might be that falling asleep was an act of avoidance. Losing one's virginity was not like having a tooth pulled, as I had tried to tell myself; it was being a citizen of a new country, a new person forced in among the motley others I was: scholar, aesthete, writer, the woman in a coarse country cloak who devoted her virgin talents to a greater one, like Dorothy Wordsworth to brother William, like Mary Lamb, when she wasn't mad, to brother Charles. What would happen to my life with Davy when I became an experienced nonvirgin? In spite of my failed, clumsy foray into Harlem, I didn't want to be a "lay," a thing I might become, a thing of submissiveness and victimization, of being flattened and mounted, maybe spreading for someone I hardly knew. I was troubled, too, about the potential looks of Jones's elderly penis. I had never actually seen one close up (subway flashers were too fast) except on statues in the Metropolitan Museum, and in spite of the sleek white perfection of the classic bodies, or because of it, the genitals looked like pasted-on afterthoughts, brutish clusters inappropriate to the androgynous grace of these demi-gods. If that's what they looked like on Apollo, imagine the kind of grotesquerie an old man dangled from the bottom of his belly.

And Jones had let me fall asleep; his dozens of allusions and illustrations, his spate of poetic clichés, might have been *his* avoidance. As soon as I opened my eyes after a gentle nudge from him, he began to say he had chosen not to disturb me because I looked so much like a sleeping wood sprite, a dryad of ancient myths. Under my fake smile of flattered pleasure, there was a silent grumbling: "Shut up, please, shut up." Yet I kept nodding and smiling as we started back, trying to look responsive and intelligent while he went on, this time roaming in Greek mythology, singing the glorious life of Zeus, who could become a swan, a bull, anyone, anything, and cause any nymph to become enamored of him and eager for mating. By the time he reached the cruel, destructive jealousy of wife Juno, we had arrived at Marian's house. We both put on sly, contented smiles as we opened the door. Marian was alone, sitting on the edge of her couch, holding a book. To her questioning smile I answered nothing, torn between a light regret at having disappointed her and the pleasure of having foiled her. Jones said I had fallen asleep with too much breeze and sun and looked so enchanting among the trees that he didn't want to wake me. Another time; there was no rush and shouldn't be about these matters, should there?

A later weekend we were taken on a long drive by the Russian in his rattling, last-breath car, Marian, Jones, and I, to a beach where the tide was very low and the water shallow for a long

distance into the sea. As I walked into the water, Jones came to
me, put his arm around my waist, said something about Ibsen's
Lady from the Sea, and paced our steps to a slow, ritualistic
walk, suggesting that we might keep going forever until the sea
covered us. A sucker for any poetic idea, any extreme gesture, I
was almost ready to try. Having grown familiar with his hyperbole, however, I knew at the same time that he was no more
interested in drowning, however poetically, than I. The long
solemn progress, as to a temple, stopped when we were out of
sight of our friends on the beach and still only waist deep in the
water. He turned toward me and kissed me fully and breathlessly long. Still holding me, he pulled his head back to look
searchingly into my eyes. The act had to be played out, so I kept
my eyes centered on his, hoping they suggested something profound and moving. I couldn't keep it up as long as he did; that
other self, my doppelgänger (a word I had borrowed from
Schubert), was standing a few feet away, saying I looked like a
dolt and why the lying gestures? I wasn't lying, I answered. This
was an attractive game I might never play again. Where would I
find another Jones? And anyhow, now was not the time to hurt
the old man's feelings, fake as they might possibly be, as fake as
mine. As my eyes dropped, they stopped at his wrinkled neck,
slid down to the sag of breast, down to the belly pouch slanting
sadly like a half-filled sack, down to the back of his hand, which
carried a purple tree of thickened veins. And he talked too, too
damned much. In spite of Marian's injunctions and recommen-
dations and the important fact that Jones might be the instru-
ment of a college scholarship, as Marian had half promised, it
was not this one who would lead me to Orphic joys. Davy would
do me for the time being; to hell with the technicalities. They
would come, I was sure, sometime.

In spite of his frustrating experience with me, Jones didn't
altogether lose interest in my butterfly-blue veins under my
peach-down skin, in his phrase. He dashed at me unexpectedly,
some months after the walk into the sea, in the lobby of Carnegie Hall, where we were separately attending a performance of

Bach's B Minor Mass. Behind him stood the woman who paid for his rent and, apparently, for his concert tickets, looking around, carefully not observing us as he fervidly kissed my hands and face. A few days later I received a letter from him, an elaborate tapestry of words about the Lady from the Sea, about striding into the belly of the Amniotic Mother Sea together, about a long kiss that was a mystic seal, about the exultant celebration of Nature and man in Bach's music. The mingling of Ibsen, Bach, the sea, the long kiss, the birthing fluid—the extravaganza of phrases—was beyond my patience, old-fashioned and ludicrous to the aficionado of stark Hemingway prose and sharply etched Frost poetry I then was. Enclosed with the letter were two tickets at five dollars each for a weekend festival and dance in his Connecticut community. An attached note explained that the tickets were a gift, one for a boy I might want to bring along, and not to worry about accommodations; he had made all arrangements.

Youth trampling middle age, shrieking in triumph, it may unconsciously have been, but it seemed natural—I didn't question or hesitate for a moment—to show the letter to Marian. She was my closest friend, my teacher in all things important, the begetter of my friendship with Jones, and should be interested in the letter and the tickets. I dashed to her lunchroom table, waving the letter, on the very day I received it. The letter didn't seem to impress her. She skimmed it quickly, muttering, "The usual seduction junk," but the tickets flung her into an astonishing fury, a storm I would never have suspected in my ideal of the cultivated, worldly woman, the revered mentor. Like a coarse market woman, like the immigrant peasants of my childhood when they threatened their kids, Marian's face became distorted and poured out sour words in a harsh shrillness. "He sent you two tickets, two, for free? He never spent a cent on me or Lydia or Maggie! And now for a snot of sixteen he uses the money we give him, hard-earned money! And don't think he'll find a bed for the boy you're supposed to invite; he'll put you in his own bed and let the boy sleep in a cold cellar! Ten dollars! Ten dollars! I just bought him an imported shirt for ten dollars and was going to buy him an English raincoat for his birthday." She spat out at me, "You buy him the goddamned raincoat! Take my place, see if you can support him and his lordly tastes on your part-time pennies." I protested that I didn't want the tickets, I had no one to go with, I didn't want to go, I didn't even have the bus fare. She didn't listen but kept spitting venom on him and me.

The next morning, when we met in the hall, she wouldn't speak to me. She turned away from me in the lunchroom and rushed by when I waited for her after school. She never spoke to me again. Distraught and bewildered, the earth dissolving under my feet, the college scholarship she and Jones were to arrange fading from sight, I wrote her explaining that I had not seen or been in touch with Jones except for that chance encounter in Carnegie Hall. She knew everything that had gone on between us and nothing but words really had, I had no wish to become one of his harem, I didn't want to sleep with him, ever, I was not going to the festival—had returned the tickets, in fact—and I couldn't understand why she was so angry with me for an act of Jones's. I had not meant to hurt her and was deeply sorry if I had. I would be grateful if she explained to me just what it was I had done to make her hate me so. She didn't answer the letter and I cut school several times during the next two weeks, mainly not to meet her and see her turn her head away. Afraid of the hazards of cutting, however, I returned to school, avoiding the lunchroom, the sections of hall and stairways near her classroom. I went to school early and left late to avoid meeting her in the street.

She had in several ways given me a Promised Land and had taken it away, leaving me abandoned, foreign to myself and my surroundings. No more theater and Italian mussels, no more artbooks and operatic records, no more verbal cadenzas about sex, no more the feeling of being a cherished child at the same time that I was a grown-up among grown-ups. Who would care what I thought of the design of an Art Nouveau chair, if I read

Montaigne, if I knew what Heywood Broun had said that morning, whether I had money for a pack of cigarettes? I became again the raw armature of the piece of sculpture she seemed for a while to have been so vigorously shaping. Who would be the next armature? What would happen to her life with Jones? Would she leave him because of me? What happened to the woman who scorned jealousy?

Eve expelled from Paradise, with Davy-Adam at my side when he wasn't working, I began to explore the city: streets of the Lower East Side Joe had not taught me, the Greek flower market in the West Twenties, and to the east, restaurants Moroccan, Lebanese, Armenian, wafting spicy odors. We learned the Czechoslovakian, the Hungarian, the German craftshops of fine cabinetmaking and violin repair in the East Seventies and Eighties, and the red-checkered tablecloths in their kitchenlike restaurants. We found the Ukrainians with their blouses and painted eggs and honey on Seventh Street. We walked across the Brooklyn Bridge toward stately unused warehouses and, above, old houses and their magnificent views of Manhattan. And back and forth, back and forth, on the Staten Island ferry and the Fifth Avenue bus. Once cloistered in the ghettos of home and school, we were becoming tireless, impassioned New Yorkers. The incomprehensible world of Marian faded slowly, gradually; pictures I saw were often those she had taught me, music I heard was hers, books I read had her stamp on their pages, and from place to place in my restless youth I carried a small bilingual leather-bound volume of the poems of Heinrich Heine that she had given me. I still have it.

7. HUNTER COLLEGE

Through an agent I despised, viperous Ruthie, I was pushed along my peripatetic journey from bed to bed, room to room, to a small room on Commerce Street in the Village. I was quite contented with its modest virtues—hooks for my undemanding wardrobe, the two shelves that held my underclothing and books—and particularly pleased with the small, arrogant mouse who would stare at me from the curtain rod as I stared at him; banging, shoe-throwing had little effect: he left only when he had enough of me. My landlady, Mrs. Essen, was the handsome, graceful mother of vicious, ugly Ruthie, the source of the most poisonous gossip in James Monroe, designed to knife friendships she envied. The girl lived with her father, hating her mother and her stepfather ("She isn't really married to that shit, she's his mistress and the kid is illegitimate"—Ruthie speaking) and especially her radiant bright-haired younger half-sister. What might have been Ruthie's room became mine, for a small fee and the obligation to sit with the little girl when the couple went to the Yiddish theaters on Second Avenue and later sat with their actor friends in the Café Royale, across the street from the most influential theater. We all got along very well, I often treated as a guest, invited to listen to the poetry readings of Mr. Essen, a director, and a failed poet. The Yiddish

of his verse was simple enough to understand. What was difficult were his narrow fields of simile: children, women's eyes,
small flowers, were all *ziggalach*, young goats—a disconcerting
dullness as I made unfair comparisons with the great Romantic
poets.

On New Year's Eve Mrs. Essen asked if Davy and I would like
to accompany her to the Café Royale, where we would celebrate
with her husband and their friends of the theater. We eagerly
would and did. The deep, wide room was dazzlingly lit, as noisy
as a market and as brilliantly, gaudily colored as a Gypsy camp.
We recognized a few of the actors as Essen guests and as Second
Avenue billboard posters, all of them in full stage makeup,
cheeks hectic, eyes blazing. Several of the women wore large
embroidered Spanish shawls with deep tassels that they tossed,
stroked, and wound around their crimson-nailed fingers. One
famous tragedienne wore a tall, blaring-red turban; another,
with heavily kohl-circled eyes, sported a yellowed ermine cape-
let, her hands buried in its matching Anna Karenina muff. They
called and waved and hugged each other and ran from table to
table to exchange laughter and fervent affection. Davy and I
were introduced to a few people, who kissed us roundly, admired our youth and beauty, then turned back to praise magnificent performances, superb costumes, imaginative direction, admiring each other extravagantly. Left on our own after the
initial welcomes, Davy and I made our way through the darting
bodies, the tassels, the furs, the dashing hats and billowing
neckerchiefs, to the crowded table of a quiet, smiling group
listening to one droll-faced man. He was the famous journalist
of whom we had heard, who could maintain a conversation or a
long monologue on almost any subject in rhymed couplets in
Yiddish, quite a feat. He was adroit, funny, and gracious
enough to invent a lilting set of couplets for us "rosy baby
lovers."

It was a happy time. The mouse stayed faithful, Davy was
always welcome, I had my very own keys. Except for sitting with
the little golden girl once in a while, I was free, after school and

work hours, to be an envied denizen of the Village, to buy a couple of cookies at Sutter's on Bleecker Street late at night as they came out of the redolent ovens. I could stare in at parties through the long windows of Horatio Street, imagine myself behind the flowers and the New Orleans ironwork on Eleventh Street near Fifth, drop in to talk with the Sicilian shoemaker on Carmine Street who baked orange rind on the top of a small stove to rid the narrow shop of the smells of glue and polish. I could buy apples at Balducci's broad fruit stall at the corner of Greenwich and Sixth and stand across from the women's prison on Tenth Street hoping to catch a significant criminal happening or at least a roundup of prostitutes. I could walk in Washington Square Park on a Sunday morning to watch the children on the swings and slides or sit down with a book near a young man rocking a baby carriage, estimating how long it would take him to ask what I was reading and pull a conversation out of that. Several times conversation with men no longer very young— late thirties or forty—turned to nostalgic, dreamy narratives of how they played in their childhood parks, in their streets, and what movie stars they worshiped, accounts that were both wistful views of a lost world and a gift, a gift of a kind of lovemaking, subtle but unmistakable.

For another sort of small lovemaking I could go to the cafeteria on Sheridan Square to find a saturnine young composer I had once grappled with at a party. He always sat at a window seat, covering lined music paper with rapid notes and quick strokes of bars, waving the paper about from time to time to help the notes dry and, my bitchiness told me, to gather as much attention to himself and his art as was possible from a cafeteria seat. Since our grappling evening, he knew that the attack direct wouldn't work with me. A newer tack was meant to work on my sensibilities, my sympathy. He told me in one manuscript-waving cafeteria conversation that his hearing was growing dull, dim, not as sharp as a musician's should be. I knew, of course, that Beethoven was deaf and couldn't hear his last great works at all, didn't I? And the same was happening to him, he was afraid. But if Beethoven could live and work in deafness, so could he. The lips quivered a bit, the eyelids drooped, as if to hold back tears. I would have been deeply moved had I not witnessed this act once or twice before, and seen him respond to seductive pianissimo voices when he chose to.

I had the small conquests, a vivacious neighborhood, a room of my own, money, meager but my own, a boyfriend of my own, a life of my own, responsible only to those for whom I felt responsible, and they were few. I would always be unassailable, unconquerable. I would never die.

Life's rains washed out my lovely parade. Ruthie the viper had to leave her father's house; his new wife wouldn't have her another day, the lying little bitch. Her mother dreaded having her but had no choice. In genuine sorrow compounded with many fears, my landlady with the vulnerable face explained that I had to go. Expulsion from Paradise I could brook but not expulsion from my vivid and, at that time, only a shade self-conscious Village. An ad in the local paper—*The Villager*, I think—led me to "a loft on historic Bank Street" (historic because the banks of the eighteenth century were moved up here for the summer months when yellow fever attacked the crowded city to the south). The loft was a papery attic, cut into three or four segments. My room, at three dollars a week, was wedged into the slant of a steep roof gable, offering low snug shelter for the shaky cot and a few feet of space to sit and stand in normally. My neighbor, a taciturn woman who appeared to keep the nine-to-five hours of a job, seemed to live in the same arrangement at the opposite slope of the gable. We were the elite of the attic. On either side of our closed rooms there were open areas like large playpens, furnished with pads on the floor and surrounded by slats that marked territorial borders. It was one of my firm principles not to complain, to be an endurer like my mother, and it suited me to tell my friends amusing stories about life in the cold attic, like that of the artists in *La Bohème*. I tried valiantly to be charmed, and when I couldn't manage that, tried to warm myself in my cloak of independence. Independence turned another face, fearsome unsafety, when I was molested by my crib neighbors. One was a woman who seemed never to dress, although there was some clothing hanging on her territorial slats, but stayed wrapped in a tattered comforter. She must have been half mad with loneliness, with no space to move in, and chose me as confidante and playmate. She stood at the head of the tall stairs when she heard my step or outside the communal toilet when she thought I was in it, to grab me for stories of past riches and glamorous travels—the commonest collection of fantasies. I would listen for a while, then, on the excuse of having to leave soon for a job, would pull her insistent hand from my arm. The encounters were only mildly disconcerting until she began to suggest, with lumpish, embarrassing coyness, that I spend the wet November nights with her, cuddle under the blankets together and keep cozy and warm.

She could accept no, however, unlike the large drunken man in the other crib, who would bang on my door, turn and turn the doorknob at all hours of the night, calling, "Let me in, pretty baby, I just wanna give you a drink and a kiss." Between wary avoidance of the woman, the sleepless noisy nights, and fear that the drunk might be able to force my door open, I felt myself sinking and sinking, and finally sank into a racking cough and a high fever. It had never occurred to me that I could be ill and might need help, need someone to buy food and medicines for me—to take care of me. If I could leave my bed to telephone—if the landlord would let me use the hall phone near his kitchen—whom would I call? Not Davy, who was in school, or at work in a place whose number I didn't know; nor friends, who had no telephones. Certainly not my mother; it would be another confession of frailty and I had to be indomitable. The drunk kept banging on the door, the blanket-woman kept following me to the toilet; it was the taciturn working woman who brought me cans of soup, already heated, several times. The amorphous days crept by, punctuated by the night noise and the toilet encounters, until, early one morning of no classes, Davy came. After a distressed look at my disheveled hair, my damp pasty face, he burst into tears. As if his tears were a flood that washed away my fortitude, I began to cry, too, as I had not cried since I was a very young child. He said he would quit school and find a full-time job to keep us. I sobbed no, and where would he find a job with so many experienced people out of work? Anyhow, one incident of the flu or pneumonia or whatever it was I had shouldn't change the course of his plans. Whatever we decided, I couldn't stay in that cold attic, with those crazies, he said. Still crying, he packed my books and clothing in the old suitcase Marian had once given me; still crying, I washed and dressed and pulled a comb through my matted hair. We knew nothing of emergency services in hospitals. With St. Vincent's Hospital nearby and Bellevue not too far away, we walked, wobbling, to the subway and after a number of exhausting stairways and changing platforms, arrived at his mother's house. Davy, usually tactful and engaging in his approach to everyone, said curtly as his mother stared at me, "She's staying here until she's better. She can use the living room couch. You won't have to do anything. I'll take care of her and I'll pay you next week's wages for her food."

Davy didn't have to take care of me; his father did when Davy was in school or working. Being long unemployed, as I had noticed among the fathers of several friends, seemed to silence and emasculate them and they became quiet, slow-moving old women. Davy's father seemed to like serving me, urging me to eat. I ate as little as a convalescing young appetite could manage of the two- or three-day-old bread that was bought cheaply at a local bakery and the improvisations on bones, stock of wilted soup greens, beans, and homemade noodles—types of minestrone, the classic poverty dish—that Davy's mother cooked up in large kettles. She saved a little each time to use as the base for the next invention, which might be a stew of carrots, onions, and potatoes, strengthened by another bone or two wheedled from the local butcher. I knew that Depression was the country we lived in, but my father was never out of a job; we had fresh rolls and generous helpings of meat and chicken, and my mother bought her soup greens fresh and perky.

Under Davy's father's care and the comfort of hearing ordinary human voices around me—children fighting in the tenement hallway, the dumbwaiter rattling its call for garbage in the kitchen, the slap of playing cards on the dining table—and the resilience of seventeen, I turned my attention to the matter of conquering the squat Victorian Gothic world of Hunter College.

Besides the illness and unhappiness of Bank Street, it was a trying time. Davy carried too heavy a load of courses and jobs and I had drawn tight the struggle to graduate from high school with my English medal, in spite of my truant's record and the anger of the physical training department en masse, which considered me the most recalcitrant, unathletic student they had ever encountered, probably a young Bolshie, certainly one of those know-it-all Yid kids. They were all, in my prejudiced view of them, humorless, foursquare, anti-thinking, what now might be called "jocks," with thin *goy* hair and thick chins. As soon as I learned the word "fascist" I was delighted to cover them with it. Since Marian and Jones, the androgynous Pygmalion to my cloddish Galatea, were no longer in my life and there was no scholarship on the horizon, I had to do my college education on my own.

I had to, to please my mother, to apologize to her for having been so many times so merciless, including the most recent act, refusing to attend my graduation exercises, denying my mother the pleasure of seeing her firstborn celebrated in the ranks of the well-educated. I had to, to show my father that in spite of him, I could make it. I had to show Marian I could, without her help; to thank Mr. Brandon and the English and music departments, who had been so steadily encouraging. I had to because of the light mutual crush between me and a history teacher who looked like one of the young officers in *The Three Sisters,* he insistent that I had to go on to college. I had to because, having dragged my independent and erratic way through high school, I deserved it, confident that I could drag my independent and erratic way through college.

The only college I could afford was Hunter, of the City College system, then virtually free. The only possible way I could be admitted, however, was to satisfy its requirement of five semesters of high-school mathematics, none of which I had had in James Monroe, all of which had to be conquered successfully in one semester. With the understanding permission of the authorities of Washington Irving High School, I registered for the five courses. For someone whose mind shattered at the sight of numbers and the sound of the word "math," it was an order to climb Mount Everest. Sines and cosines, theorems, numbers into letters and vice versa, were a return to the incomprehensible kabalistic exercises I tried to learn, with no success at all, from derby-hatted, fine-fingered Mr. Roth of my Bronx childhood. For a while, the mingling of algebra, geometry, and intermediate geometry, swirling like Poe's maelstrom in my mind, forced thoughts of giving up, of running away and maybe— doing what? But with Davy's help and an unexpected sudden view of algebra as rather simple puzzles, and geometry as strict abstract pictures, it all fell into place. The finest irony of that time was that my high math grades, plus my English medal made me acceptable to competitive Hunter.

According to the WPA *New York City Guide,* one of the finest works of the Depression, Hunter was originally the Normal College of the City of New York, established in 1870, its name changed, when its scope broadened in 1914, to honor the founder, Thomas Hunter. This indelibly remarkable school-menagerie gave me and my friends—or tried earnestly to— what might be called a quality education, requiring a great deal more of its students than is asked there now and in many other colleges. Several faculties required of their seniors studies that are today considered graduate courses, and everyone had to spend some time in all the major fields of learning, from the classics to integral calculus. The tacit ideal was to make cultivated women of us, and to a good degree the Hunter of my years succeeded, giving us solid expertise in one field, useful or at least entertaining knowledges in several others, and, best of all, numerous frames of reference which left us with lively curiosity and many threads to follow as and if we chose to.

In its change from teacher-training school to liberal arts college, Hunter still retained a faint tinge of semicloistered female academy (or was it nuns' school?), strongest when it floated out of the offices of several controlling officials with searching mother superior manners, who were looking into the moral *faiblesse* of that girl or the other rumored to be leading an "irregular" life. Another lingering vestige was the paucity of male professors. Of the few men teachers, I remember fairly well two, both young and each in his way quite attractive, particularly to the many vulnerable, love-starved girls who had few or no dates and hadn't the luck to be bound, like myself, at least for the time being, in a solid partnership with a boy. One man was pale and enameled, with a high, Romantic poet's brow and the strayed lock favored by nineteenth-century engravers. Titillating whispers, freighted with words like "affair" and "divorce," normally the property of movie magazines, greatly enhanced his allure. I never had a class with him, never saw him as seductive, and furthermore was protected by my more advanced age (a year or two older than my classmates, thanks to the semester of math classes and six months as interoffice messenger with B. Altman and Company before I came to Hunter, and the precocity of some of the Quiz Kids who entered before they were sixteen) and my attachment to Davy. I no longer had any use for crushes and consequently found the other young professor, in the German Department, with whom I did have classes, interesting but not especially lovable. Nor did I want to run off with him to the Black Forest, of which he spoke with such *Heimweh,* nor did I dream, as some classmates did, that he would leave his robust German wife and blond children for me and that we would elope to Italy—maybe Bologna, maybe Padua—where he would teach German literature and I English literature and we would become the twin stars of an intellectual community that walked hand in hand with Browning and Goethe.

He was thin, angular, and moved jerkily, like a stick doll. His hair was spiky and willful, winging in all directions from his skull, a proper frame for the spiky mind and the witty, angular face with high cheekbones that pushed at slanted green eyes; a snaggletooth glimmered from his wide-lipped, mobile mouth. He was innovative and quirky in his methods and his opinions, which took on excitement as he dashed restlessly from one corner of the room to another, ridiculing the views of George Bernard Shaw and extolling the misanthropy of Strindberg in the European drama course I had with him. For improving the quality of the German in his language classes, he invented rhymes, riddles, and crossword puzzles, rather like the painless learning devices of Dr. Huebner in high school.

Some years later he left Hunter. He had, I was told, gone back to Germany to help in Hitler's Conquest of the World. This was difficult to absorb for a while, since he had appeared liberal, and was never known to have made any sort of anti-Semitic remark, though the opportunities were many in a school whose population included a large number of Jewish girls. But whether we believed it or not, the Professor O.K. whose voice we recognized on the radio spewing anti-American, anti-British, and particularly anti-Semitic propaganda was our erstwhile bright, swift, querulous man of culture, our stellar example of the cultivated European.

It was difficult to explain to Davy and other non-Hunter friends why I was registered in several German courses—a German major to a biology minor, in spite of my English medal —rather than concentrating on English classes. The simple fact of the matter was that examinations for English teachers had been suspended for an indefinite time—there were too many applicants—and in Hunter, at least, the English major, the base for teaching English, had become a difficult goal to achieve and maintain. It was a complicated process, too dull to explore in detail, that had some resemblance to climbing peaks which grew higher and higher until the atmosphere one breathed was quite rarefied. Or one could compare the achievement to beholding the Holy Grail after a long, wearying quest. We few knights who had made the full journey were rewarded with a juicy variety of arcane courses, a fine field for snobbishness: who else but we few could speak Chaucerian Middle English, quote long passages of Anglo-Saxon poetry, speak knowingly of Diarmuid and Gráinne, early Irish lovers in the Tristan and Isolde line, could write essays on King David as a mixed-up modern neurotic?

Who had the background for such dreams as mine? One night I was a noble lady of medieval times named Marguerite, the white daisy that was purity, the flower of the Virgin Mary. I wore a gold brocade dress, broad at the waist to accommodate the Second Coming; my feet were enfolded in soft leather, like gloves, on my head a tapering wimple from which floated a long silken veil. Accompanied by ladies-in-waiting wearing flower chaplets, I seated myself on a thronelike chair placed for me in the company of other nobles, at the side of the field of jousting that fronted my castle. Several knights tilted, thrusted, unhorsed each other. Then my lover and his adversary came to the field. He was not altogether my lover, but my lover in the manner of courtly love—the man who wrote me love songs, who vowed eternal fealty and protection, who made me deep obeisances and looked long at me from sea-blue Saxon eyes. As he rode toward the center of the field, I detached the white silken veil from my wimple and handed it to a handmaiden to give to him. My knight attached it to his sleeve, publicly acknowledging our profound union. While he turned and loosed and held his steed in a masterly display of horsemanship, while he urged his shining lance swiftly and skillfully at his adversary's cuirass and helmet, my veil—my spirit of love—swirled and darted and rode high above him in victory.

A second dream was less simple, less direct. I was a young

monk, riding a swift horse past churches, past palaces, past vineyards, to bring an important message from the court of the Visconti of Milan to the Scaligeri of Verona. The message was actually an object, a small revolver recently invented by a Frenchman, an invaluable weapon and ornament for any gentleman, lighter than a sword and more deadly, and possibly useful in warfare. The Visconti thought they could buy the Frenchman, then kill him and keep all his little weapons for themselves, wielding a great advantage over their friends and neighbors. The dream then swam into details of tapestries and paintings, the Venetian velvets and fine lace on the court ladies, and the tight doublets and hose of court pages. (The analytic suggestions here are not too arcane, and anyone is welcome to them.)

The same rich brew may have existed in other departments —I'm inclined to think not, if only from the width and depth of the field and the variety of minds it attracted—but our particular cluster of female English professors of several ages, several styles of manners and mannerisms, degrees of chic and raggedness, the earthbound and those who flew with the high, wild geese, made a fascinating scholastic display. One smart, guarded young woman who had come from a school with an awesome name left Hunter after two or three years; we decided that an orderly Harvard professor had carried her off to an ivy-covered New England retreat, where, instead of sexing, they would read Milton to each other. She was a cold and discontented young woman—as one began to know her—who had no impressive enlightenments and yet was ambitious, it seemed, to become a memorable, legendary professor, like George Lyman Kittredge of Harvard, for instance. Impelled to guide us into adornments of English literature, she asked whether some of us might like to sing Elizabethan madrigals and write masques in the style of Ben Jonson, outside of class time. I was the only student to arrive at the appointed time and place for discussion of these projects. As we waited fruitlessly for others to arrive, she uttered a few sharp words, pointing out that we

were called, and properly, "Hunter girls," while Radcliffe
taught "women," as did Barnard and Bryn Mawr. After that
insulting afternoon, I only mildly insulted, she humiliated, I
became her favorite, but soon fell among the contemptible
"girls" when she caught my sneaky, critical look as she read
"mastiff witch" for "mastiff bitch" in a Coleridge poem. She
knew I knew she was bowdlerizing, a cowardly act, a desecration
of Coleridge and poetry, according to my unforgiving priggish-
ness and wise-guy shots at teachers. She gave me an A nevertheless and I pushed on to the next perilous journey of the En-
glish-major quest.

It is impossible to describe the specific subject—purportedly
a branch of English literature—of another instructor, who lived
in an empyrean blue that scorned definitions and limits. She was
small and elderly, with thin white hair and eyes that looked like
pale grapes in sour cream; her vague, fluty voice matched her
milky eyes and hair. She consorted with ghosts and spirits in a
nebulous world through which she wanted us to wing with her. I
was perfectly willing to adventure with this sweet mother of the
Mad Hatter, but my pragmatic smart friends insisted on con-
crete proofs of the phenomena that were her familiars. After
being pushed and buffeted, she stiffened her eighty-five pounds
and proudly challenged them with "Prove me the airplane!"
leaving her adversaries wide-eyed and mute. No one answered,
but I was, and still am, delighted with her. Another professor,
visiting from Ireland for one year, held classes in her literature
from the legends of Cuchulain to the plays of Shaw. (We managed to erase troublesome Oscar Wilde entirely.) The tall,
gaunt woman with dark hair and ravaged face looked to my
romantic eye like pictures I had seen of Yeats's rebel love, Maud
Gonne. To our meager knowledge of Irish history and early
literature, knowing Ireland mainly through its treacly songs,
she added the revelation that these songs were "fustian" masks.
"I'll Take You Home Again, Kathleen" or vows to Mavour-
neen or Macushla, seemingly love songs, were actually promises
of rebellion against the English, promises that Ireland would be

free. Repeating the words of the songs, she grew increasingly proud and defiant. Reviling the greedy, ruthless English and recounting the rape of magnificent Irish forests decreed by Elizabeth I, she would burst into tears and weep as if she were a present witness and victim. I later heard the same present pain in the trembling voices of American Indians and refugee Jews.

There were also a few pragmatic professors who didn't scorn to pick up a stimulating idea from a student's paper to be used as her own contribution to a learned journal. What student ever saw the professional quarterlies? And if by some outrageous chance she did and found her teacher's article, who would believe an accusation of plagiarism directed by a snotty kid against a respected scholar? Then there were the foreign exchange instructors, poised pieces of exotica slumming among us. The German Department had imported a pleasant young woman who looked somewhat like Greta Garbo; she imitated the hairdos, the makeup and clothing, but did not know how to garner the magic. My course with her in Schiller and Goethe was a series of papers invariably marked, "Ideas outstanding, grammar repellent." In spite of my contemptible grammar, we became quite friendly, she soon eager to have me meet the young millionaires who were her friends. They really were millionaires, or close enough, as I learned from having dinner with her and a smitten young man who languished in love like a heroine in a Victorian novel. After dinner in a restaurant famous for its Pimm's Cup (whose nectars I didn't appreciate), where I gorged on duck with fruit sauce for the first time in my life, we stopped at his house to leave a message for the caretaker. It was neither a house nor a mansion but some unreal literary thing in a foreign language, a *schloss,* a *château,* a *palazzo,* a castle out of chivalric stories. It was an endlessness of dark rubbed woods, of marble floors and ruby brocades surrounded by formal gardens and a park where white classical statues postured in the pale moonlight. Lisl asked me as we walked in the garden whether I thought she should marry this young man; could she live, did I think, in such a big, rich place with so many servants? Would his parents accept her, a foreigner and, although of an old line whose blood ran in the veins of a medieval emperor, not very rich? With the arrogance of inexperience I advised her freely, in which direction I cannot remember.

Whether she married this one or not, she thought I, too, should snag a young millionaire. Not all of them were afraid, as their fathers were, of Roosevelt and his liberal cohorts. Some of them were eager to join the shaping century of the "common man." Someone like myself, a girl of the people, a brave, independent spirit, Jewish, poor, and "interesting," might attract a few of the boys who were bent on developing broad, tolerant, contemporary minds. A few days after the visit to the house of the patinas and brocades (with a stop in an implausible cut-velvet toilet) and the stroll through the cold, naked marbles, Lisl's friend invited me and a few cavaliers to a yachting party. As usual, my impulse was to run fast in the other direction. This was too foreign an experience, too demanding. What would I talk about? What did I know about polo ponies, about low, whippy roadsters and yachts, except from the pictures I saw in the society section of the newspapers? What lies would I have to invent to placate Davy? What would I wear? I had one cotton dress and one bathing suit, both shabby. Or was I supposed to appear shabbily working-class, and talk about Mike Gold and Floyd Dell, and tell the pretty young men about "radical" movements about which I had strong feelings and feeble information? The impulse to accept was equally strong, as usual, and I accepted, borrowing ten dollars from a friend to buy a classy dress in Klein's and borrowing a bathing suit, quite new and slinky, from my classmate Dinah, like me generously padded. As I pulled on the bathing suit in one of the Hunter bathrooms to make sure it fit, I saw myself stretched like a houri on embroidered silken cushions, shadowed from the refulgent sun by a canopy of peacock feathers. Gathered around me were adoring young men in bright-buttoned blazers and visored yachting caps. They all had straight small noses and clean, straight, white teeth.

In the miscellany that is my biography, there frequently appears a caricature of bags of gold and jewels running away from me fast, like Virtue fleeing the Foul Fiend in old prints. If money courts me (a friend whispers that this smitten gentleman is Mr. OPEC), a bit uncertain of foot and tongue as we all are at a party or opening, if it charms, beckons, invites, glistens, pulls me into an alcove to make firm arrangements for getting together alone—the first seductive, treacherous phrase in the vocabulary of love and lamentation—it is sure, before telephone numbers can be exchanged, to trip on a large ashtray and so surprise its balance and alcoholic content that it passes out, never to be heard from again. My first such experience of swift abandonment by golden bejeweled butterflies was propelled by Lisl, unwillingly, I prefer to think. For days before the outing, I had been gliding into the world of privilege, preparing to abandon Klein's for Bergdorf's, to buy a bathing suit when I had a whim for one, or seven or eight. Exquisitely dressed, adorned with discreet baubles of emeralds and pearls devised centuries ago by Italian goldsmiths, I would drop soft clatters of chips on the gaming tables of Monte Carlo and Deauville. I would return to Park Avenue on the *France,* entertaining distinguished statesmen in my suite, ordering champagne and caviar in perfect French.

This moving-picture version of the high life was blanked two days before the outing by a phone call from Lisl. She had had too much sun the past weekend and was now in the hospital being treated for burns; with much regret she had backed out, for both of us, from the yachting party. Before I could find out which hospital or whether I could do anything for her, she hung up. I didn't hear from her until two months later. A note from Germany informed me that family matters had demanded her immediate presence after she left the hospital. She was returning to America in the fall and would be in touch with me. I saw her only once again, and then in a society page, as the splendidly dressed wife of the importunate suitor I had met. Nowhere for me to go but back off the movie screen and into the favorite fantasies—in spite of Davy, who, I somehow knew, would not remain my *life*—of cold, gallant pennilessness in a garret as the helpmeet of a great artist or writer, maybe ultimately to do something famous of my own, like Mary Shelley. I gave up the Mainbocher silks for a long gown hand-embroidered in designs from the *Book of Kells*, maybe like that of the wife of noble William Morris and the inamorata of his friend Dante Gabriel Rossetti. All she and I had in common was a wild thatch of hair, hers black and passionate, mine the color of straw and hay, the unfortunate colors of bucolic innocence, but I wanted her place. Not with Rossetti, though I envied the sonnets he wrote her, but with her suffering giant husband, who would forget Jane's cruelty in the nest I would build around him and the beautiful houses which I would help him design when I wasn't editing sheets for our Kelmscott Press. Or, quite possibly, I would, like several intrepid British ladies, wander in the Judean wilderness with a tribe of Bedouins. Or I would live in a black felt tent with a group of Kurds and eat yak flesh with them, dressed in bright bands of yak wool, with big dangles of glittering stones around my neck.

While I was rising and falling with Lisl there wasn't much time or care for my Hunter companions. Now I was thrust back among them and listening to much talk about a new crush that had smitten a number of them. She was a teacher of zoology, an energetic, dark young woman with a sturdy walk and an unabashed, immoderate voice. I didn't like her earthbound looks or her brisk, efficient manner as she marched through the halls. I had no classes with her and my information was secondhand, often delivered in exaltations, young saints adoring the Virgin. "She understands so much, she's so friendly and informal. You can tell her anything, everything." "I've been invited to her house again, next week. The last time I went with Mary and she gave us coffee and cake and she showed us the artbooks she brought back from Europe." (Shades of perfidious Marian, of my high school days.) "She thinks friends, girl friends, often experience emotional pulls toward each other that they don't understand, are afraid of, and resist though close friendships with girls are more satisfying than with boys—they understand each other better—and less hazardous, like pregnancy for instance." "She says men are immature, unstable, and insensitive." Developments waxed into further developments. She gave her chosen girls little gifts and little suppers, sent them on personal errands which they treated as royal honors, awed them with her wide-ranging conversation and unconventional attitudes, favored them with strokes on the cheek, on the shoulder, told them what alluring eyes and delicate hands they had.

The clay feet showed ultimately and uglily. She invited one of her adoring friends to supper, alone, to mark a special occasion, the first anniversary of their meeting. As naive Ida told it, they had bootleg wine, two or three glasses with dinner, a glass or two afterward. While they sat and talked on the couch, Miss Hennessey opened the buttons of Ida's blouse and began to stroke her shoulder and breast and pull her close. Ida tried to move away. It was a bizarre contest, as Ida described it, the sturdy woman pulling the girl toward her to be stroked and kissed; startled, embarrassed Ida squirming away and still trying to be polite with the goddess. Herself embarrassed and angry, the goddess rose, and looking down at her acolyte of the disordered blouse and frightened eyes, hissed at her, "You stupid, stupid little kike." The cult collapsed in my immediate circle, maintained only by a few strangers in short pasted-down haircuts.

8. HUNTER GIRLS

The old Hunter building at Sixty-eighth Street and Lexington Avenue had only one shelter for girls who smoked, our most forceful symbol, other than pregnancy, of freedom from parental prohibitions. This unremittingly ugly cellar, furnished with chairs and tables that had the dull utilitarian stamp of Salvation Army furniture, was rarely used by the girls who had steady habits and controlled routines. These nonsmokers, our Conservative Party, invaded the cellar—dignified by the name "Exchange"—only when they desperately needed someone's notes. Our incommodious salon was the hangout mainly of the slightly disheveled, the class-cutters; it was for gossiping, for borrowing money, and for borrowing clothing for the not too frequent date. My usual offering was a handsome old leather pocketbook given me by Laura Bergson; Stella offered her one good blouse and Liz her rabbit jacket. On Friday afternoons, we had loud calls from Anna, of the mischievous face: "Who wants my pessary? I haven't got a date this weekend," running around from table to table offering her supreme and rare gift. Since most of us were too inexperienced to wonder about fit and general usability, she frequently found takers, handing over the small, flat box with a large, benevolent gesture. One wit or another called her our "infertility goddess."

It was in the Exchange that we ate the sandwiches our mothers had forced on us in the morning or bought from a slatternly stand a five-cent bar of chocolate that would do for lunch. It was in this cellar that some of us plotted to join the City College boys who were preparing demonstrations to oust their president. Whether he merited removal, whether students could force it, we didn't know or care; it was protest, and we, particularly those firebrands who belonged to the Young Communist League or the Young People's Socialist Party, were always ready for confrontation and battle, at least verbally. The cellar was also the place for gathering a group determined to cut afternoon classes to spend several luscious hours on sparse lunch money with long-legged, soft-lipped, delectable Gary Cooper in the nice, warm, dusty, dark movie house at Sixty-eighth Street at Third Avenue. The cellar was the place where two or three of the eldest of us met to go for a couple of after-school hours to the Aquarium, a speakeasy nearby. Its name derived from the large tanks full of varicolored fish which provided the only illumination for the dim, secretive room. One of us had been taken there by an uncle, and we used his name in our version of "Joe sent us" to get in. There were few customers at three or four in the afternoon and it amused the proprietor to serve a group of schoolgirls, laden with books, the one drink over which they would sit, puffed with sophistication, until the five o'clock masculine trade began to pour in.

The money for this ultimate worldly gesture meant the sacrifice of several movie sessions, or overtime work. It wasn't come by easily, though well worth it. To earn little, to do with little, to give up one pleasure for another, was the atmosphere we breathed, our natural climate. Many of our houses held as prisoners abashed, unemployed fathers. A number of girls, though fairly well dressed—the *bella figura* syndrome—lived in apartments almost empty of furniture, the few sticks frequently moved from apartment to apartment to avoid paying rent or being shoved out on the street. Some of the fathers went to distant boroughs, where they were not known, to sell apples;

some continued sitting with vacant eyes. Rarely cold or hungry, except when I chose to test myself, to see how much cold and hunger I could withstand (as I had practiced being lame and blind in my childhood, to see how it might feel), I was aware of the meager lives of friends, who, however, didn't feel singularly deprived, too young and gallant to complain, too familiar with the parallel lives that shaped their norm. The one experience of profoundest poverty that infuriated me, made me painfully sorrowful and ashamed that I could not alter anything, nor scream and yell and protest effectively, was the slave markets that were held in front of Woolworth stores in several neighborhoods, black women facing white women who wanted a few hours of household help at the lowest possible cost. It was dreadful to watch black women outbid each other downward for the jobs: "I'll take twenty-five cents an hour." "Hey, missus, I'll work for twenty cents." Another offered herself for eighteen cents. I don't know if the bidding ever went lower; after a few moments I would run from the shameful scenes.

The group that preempted the Exchange table at which I usually sat—preempted early and held stubbornly, as others held their territories—was a kaleidoscopic mixture composed of a core of intimate friends and visitors who admired our free-form ways and nasty tongues. One girl who sat with us once in a while was the princess of a long line—on both parental sides—of dynasties of Chassidic rabbis, the Chosen of the Chosen. Malka was afraid of the marriage, with the learned scion of another dynasty of rabbis, already in negotiation. She had met him once and found him pimply and little, his black frock coat hanging limply from narrow shoulders, his earlocks thin and wispy. She sat with us, we thought, to gather as if by osmosis the strength to protest against the marriage. But she had exhausted the limits of liberty allowed her by attending Hunter College rather than a religious school. Enough. She married the little pimply Chassidic scholar, who prayed and studied at the expense of her parents—considered an honor to the family—while she shaved her auburn hair, put on an iron-ridged wig, and grew belly after belly.

Her opposite number in our gallery was a hummingbird who had been brought up in the West Indies, or possibly Cuba. Sometimes she alit wearing a tall bright turban, carrying a magic candle for an obeah ceremony she was to attend later; sometimes she sat dully, disappointed in "all that primitive crap," sans turban, sans magic candle and powders. It was a struggle, clearly, one we could neither understand nor sympathize with; crazy mixed-up kid, a curio. Then there was our fashion plate, Miriam, who lived in a large apartment full of light. Her father had a well-paying, steady job and her mother was a skilled dressmaker. The rest of us knew little about fashion and were scornful of the superficiality in the little we saw, but we could not deny style, and Miriam's clothing had style, copied by her mother from glossy magazines like *Vogue* and *Vanity Fair,* which we knew only from their covers on newsstands. There was subtle insult in the difference between our coarse skirts and cheap blouses and the soft swirl and gentle cling of her skirts, and the blouses of sculptured silk shaped like morning glories, to frame her limpid pale-brown eyes and her skin, the texture and color of antique clay, which I admired in its contrast to my ordinary white and pink. Her nails were almond-shaped, manicured by her mother, her hair a smooth cap, shaped by her mother. She was her mother's doll, as none of the rest of us had been since we were three or four, some of us never. We envied, admired, and disliked Miriam.

Esther was a studious, generous girl who had little to say but liked to listen to our babble. Suddenly she stopped coming to our table and no one saw her, in or out of classes, or at the subway station. After several weeks, Stella went to visit her and returned with a chilling story. She found Esther at home, pale, thin, and terrified at the suggestion that they go out for a walk. No, no, she couldn't go, she couldn't leave the house. Why not? Was she sick? What kind of sickness did she have? The father

shouted at her to go walking, to get out of the house, her
mother began to cry, Please, please, go out with your friend.
Esther ran into the bathroom and locked herself in and stayed
while her father banged at the door, alternately begging her to
come out and threatening her with the fire department, the
police department, who would get her out and maybe send her
to Bellevue, the current euphemism for an insane asylum. The
weeping mother told Stella that one morning Esther decided
not to go to school. No one thought anything of it, a heavy
menstrual period, probably. That same evening she canceled a
date to go to the library with a neighborhood friend. The next
day, no school, no going out anywhere, not even on an errand
around the corner. She hid in a closet, in the bathroom, when it
was suggested she leave the house. It was weeks now and they
didn't know what to do. The only agency they knew was the
Board of Health, a foreign, suspect power that might put Esther
in a crazy cell and keep her there forever. Event crowding on
event, we forgot about her after a while, but for weeks before
thought about the gap between universal, common craziness—
the *meshugge* with which we Jewish girls were often stamped and
dismissed—and her black pit of a world, like scenes of hell,
called insanity.

It was the wet, gloomy days, when the Exchange smelled of
rubber overshoes and damp coats, that wafted the densest mists
and miasmas on which to float intimate self-images at each
other. The display was often led off by a fantasy phrase spoken
in a dreamy voice by someone on the fringe of our circle, im-
pressing her way toward the center. One such contender for
our attention was a large girl, all dark gold—hair, skin, and
eyes—like girls I later saw in Greece and northern Italy. Elena's
perfection was preserved by the immobility of her Minerva face.
She rarely smiled because her teeth were short and her gums
long, and the excessive display of wet, pink flesh, marring her
Greek goddess look, tortured her. To match her immobile face
she walked with slow, measured steps toward a distant vision, a
seeress, a Sibyl, a Cassandra. The majestic stride and the digni-

fied face were dictated, she explained one gray afternoon, by the fact that she was the vessel of a special destiny; there was a pulsating, constant bubbling in her throat, a reminder that she would someday be great. How? She wasn't too good at the piano, she agreed, nor much of a writer, and the pencil sketches she scrawled were too close to ad drawings. But her throat kept bubbling, gently nudging her toward heights, great one way or another, she had no doubt, maybe as a suffragette or an actress or a great courtesan like—what was her name?—Lily Langtry.

No one else we knew had a nonstop prophetic bubble, but some of us English majors had been sufficiently seduced by books to dedicate ourselves to dreams of lives that echoed the "infinite variety" of Cleopatra; withering and staling as our grandmothers and mothers did were to be avoided at the profoundest costs. We would live heroic sorrows and great pleasures as we learned them in Shakespeare, in Greek dramas and French novels, as we learned them from the daring, tough, begging-for-the-knife-in-the-bodice Carmen. And there were the lush, toothsome Belle Époque women, all pearls, plumes, and rose satin, as introduced to us by the Goncourts and Proust. If not the Odettes, the gallant unfortunates, semi-loved and thoroughly discarded, of Zola and Dreiser, and, closer to our own time, the burners of candles at both ends: Edna St. Vincent Millay, Genevieve Taggard, Elinor Wylie.

The need to be in love or connected in some way to love also sculptured almost three-dimensional, almost in-the-flesh, Hamlets to moon over, Shelleys and Keatses to worship and mourn, Byrons to spy on in their Italian villas, to want and fear their swift words, to make despairing jealous hags of their wives and mistresses. The need for loving often moved from literary fantasy to pairings in intense friendships, charged with jealousy, with demands of constant attention and affection, with strident fighting and humbling tears. Those of us who were spectators were divided on whether the passions included overt sexuality. Were our frenetic friends possibly lesbians in the fullest sense? I somehow doubted it, but there were those who were titillated by the presence of Sapphos among us, an advanced, mysterious society, imagined as Amazons and frail, peplumed girls.

Since I was nearer self-supporting than the rest, with several jobs to run among, there were periods when I was absent, regretfully, from the gossiping marketplace of the Exchange. During my absences, a naive, crush-inspired legend attached itself to me, almost naturally for the atmosphere, stemming from my extraordinary, boundless freedom and abetted by the clouds of fantasy that painted the gray air of that cellar. As mentioned, I was at least a year older than most of my friends, had worked in the real commercial world, wandered as I would, lived as I could. No parental supervision strangled me, no mother wrung her red, wash-swollen hands over my delinquencies, no father roared that I was not to go out and to give him back his keys. The keys I had were my own, to a place that was my own. In short, I was not a girl but a woman, to be envied, and idealized, as Isadora Duncan was idealized, or Mabel Dodge Luhan and Emma Goldman. Of the glamorous universe I inhabited, touched up with lies dropped lightly about my elaborate love life—in spite of faithful Davy—concerning this poet, that actor, a painter, a composer, the girls of the small tight lives constructed a portrait of me as wildly licentious, a frenzied dancer in Dionysian revels. One imaginative portrait of the Great Kate had me dancing at night in Central Park, solo and frenetically, surrounded by a group of boys who sat in a circle, urging me on as I shimmied and swung my hips and made the take-it-off gestures of a burlesque queen. On and on I danced, the legend said, faster and more frenzied, until I suddenly dropped to the grass and burst into tears (a nice literary touch that might have been invented by the imaginative seeress of the bubble). Two boys consoled me, stroking, patting, kissing, and, in consoling, entered me. I couldn't or wouldn't say no to the other boys, so we had what later became known as a "gang bang." The realities were that I rarely danced, I never shimmied because I didn't know how, and, having not yet seen a burlesque show, knew none of its gestures. However, there was pleasure in this elevation to minor goddess, this ascension to utterly uninhibited sexpot and total free spirit. I neither confirmed nor denied the story but for a while tried to look secretive and cynical, then forgot about the whole foolish entertainment.

Gossip had a way of seeping up from the Exchange to the first-floor offices of the directors, and one day I was summoned to a meeting with a large, disconcerting woman with doughy skin who kept glancing down at the lace insert in the V of her neckline, apparently to assure herself that she was modestly covered. (The nasty eye of youth said, Never mind the modesty; no one would think of assaulting you. But pull the lace higher, real high, to cover the stippled, wrinkled flesh, so ugly.) The woman found it interesting that I lived alone. Were my parents dead, perhaps? No. Did they live outside the city, in which case I should not be attending a city college? No, my parents lived in the Bronx and I lived alone in Manhattan at the address indicated in the records. Did I live altogether alone? Or with another girl? (It was unthinkable, impossible, to ask whether I lived with a boy.) No, I lived alone, I kept saying. When she asked how I could afford it, I told her I rented a room in the house of a poor family, that I had several jobs, and that my mother sent me money. There was clearly more searching to do, but she didn't know what wedge to use or where to pierce with it. After hesitating over my record, she dismissed me. She summoned me two or three times later to answer the same questions, but the inquisition stopped when an outburst of student demonstrations at City College threatened to excite Hunter, requiring her full alertness and attention.

(Reviving Hunter brings back not only another time but, compared to university life now as I hear and read it, what seems to be part of another universe. We rarely drank, since we were products of poor, abstemious households and very few of us had access to prohibition liquor, the right of the worldly. The only drugs we knew of were the glue inhaled by some unknown boys, the opiates of Coleridge and De Quincey, and the valerian and light infusions of opium taken by Victorian ladies, among them Elizabeth Barrett Browning, who would not be broken, even by her otherwise persuasive husband, of the comforting habit. We knew about reefers—a word for marijuana that seems to have left the vocabulary—and a small few of us had tried them. But we had no wish nor the wherewithal to continue. As for the rest, we sequestered them in incomprehensible literary lives and fabled opium dens in Port Said.)

9. SUMMER, LIGHT AND DARK

Whan that Aprille with his shoures soote
The droghte of March hath perced to the roote,
And bathed every veyne in swich licour
Of which vertu engendred is the flour;
Whan Zephirus eek with his sweete breeth
Inspired hath in every holt and heeth
The tendre croppes, and the yonge sonne
Hath in the Ram his halve cours yronne,
And smale foweles maken melodye,
That slepen al the nyght with open ye . . .
Thanne longen folk to goon on pilgrimages . . .

As often, a writer I revered told me how to feel. Chaucer said to me, one fragrant spring, that I was the young sun and the tender crops and, like the wakeful birds, too merry to sleep, that I was spring, the adolescence of the year. Like myself, like Davy, our friends had also felt the pricking in their hearts that told them to plan pilgrimages for the close of the spring semester. Those with parents who would rescue them if they were stranded penniless in Broken Bow, Oklahoma, were planning to hitchhike across the country and back. The less privileged would have as their Canterburys camps in New England where they might teach swimming or crafts—a crude leather pouch for each relative. The still less blessed would tutor slow children in the city; the absolutely damned were those who had to take makeup summer courses.

Summer pilgrimages were in the planning all around us, the planners including my stalwart English student Mrs. Katz, still trying to say "the" instead of "zee" and to take the big burr out of "rrrrun"; she was going off to stay with a cousin on a farm in the Catskills, the Green Pastures of a couple of my piano pupils as well. Vito could do without me for a couple of months; his daughter would ticket the laundry bundles. Davy, too, was entering slow seasons in a couple of his jobs and eager to leave them altogether for a while. But where to go and what to do on the sixty dollars we had saved?

One late-spring holiday, we hitchhiked up to visit the Bergsons, about whom I had told Davy a good deal, describing them as an auxiliary set of parents in my fated style—mother pretty good, father terrible, except that this one knew fascinating people and owned good books; to complete the picture, a little brother and sister to take care of. During the visit Laura told us that one of her nephews had hired a patch of land for next to nothing near a filled quarry—a wonderful big swimming hole, Bill had said—from an Italian who owned the land around the quarry, a hour's walk from the Bergson summer house.

The next afternoon, toward evening, we climbed the hill toward the quarry. At the top, where the path flattened to a plateau of bushes and tangled grass, we called, "Guido, Guido," politely, tentatively, in several directions. We had been told that the Italian drank a lot of wine, didn't like company, and sometimes carried a shotgun. As we kept calling warily, not moving from our spot, a clump of bushes to our right suddenly parted and there stood the laird, broad and dirty, with a large nose and a thick mat of curly black hair. Bloodshot eyes glared into the dimming light. He had no shotgun but, instead, his hand was attached to a rope that circled the neck of a white goat. Keeping our distance from him, we asked if he had some quarry land available for July and August. We had our own tent and equipment (borrowed from one of Davy's innumerable tribe) and all we wanted of him was the rental of a piece of land and the use of the quarry. He beckoned us to follow him as he walked unsteadily, supporting himself by grasping low branches of trees and the tufts of hair on the back of his goat. The shack he led us to echoed its tenant, unkempt, disheveled, stinking of soured wine and the acrid odor of unwashed bedclothes. He poured for us jam-jar glasses of wine that was heavy and rough, the sort of wine the Italian neighbors of my childhood nursed in stained barrels each fall; it was referred to as "Guinea red." He drank from a mason jar in one hand while he caressed his goat with the other. His hand moving smoothly along her head and sides, playing absentmindedly with her nipples, he discussed our business of space and price. He thought five dollars a week would be OK. No, he didn't want any deposit. When we came to stay would be time enough to pay the first week's rent, unless we wanted to pay by the month, but it wasn't necessary. Come and see the place. We stumbled with him up a gentle hill and into a valley where there were a few tents and beyond to a dense copse that bordered a meadow on three sides and then opened on the wonderful quarry of gray Cézanne walls and blue-green water. We could pitch our tent at the far end of the meadow, Guido said. We told him it was perfect, beautiful and wondered silently if he would remember the place and the promise that it was ours.

At a slow wobbling pace, supported by whatever was at hand, including Davy's shoulder, he led us back to his cabin to sign a lease Davy improvised on a page from a child's worn copybook. First Davy signed, then he asked the old man for his signature. The Italian made a cross and then ceremoniously, with a tottering bow, gave the paper to me to sign. The paper went into a table drawer full of corks, can openers, a few spoons and forks, and other scraps of paper. We could not leave before the ritual of another glass of wine to seal our contract and new friendship. Although neither Davy nor I was accustomed to much wine and didn't like this metallic stuff, we drank and drank some more on our host's insistence, and watched him love the goat. "Cara," he called her, and "Bella." "*Vuoi fare l'amore, tesoro?*" he asked her, stroking her head, her sides, her belly, staring into her still, dumb eyes. Although I had read and heard stories about the common practice among lonely shepherds of buggering sheep and goats, I didn't think I wanted to witness the copulation of a dirty man and his four-legged lover, yet I was also pulled to stay, to see how this antique act as old as sex and loneliness was performed. Would the goat enjoy it? How would she manifest pleasure? Would she have an orgasm or was that possible only with a he-goat? Repelled and attracted, I sat awaiting developments. Suddenly realizing the potential direction of events, Davy, frowning and pale, jumped from his chair, grabbed my hand, and pulled me out of the cabin. Having had the preparation of a too-much-handled little girl, I wasn't as shocked as he. In any case, this was one more experience in a world of experiences I had to live, this only one of an infinite number of wide explorations I had promised myself. But I had to skip it because Davy was dashing down the hill yelling at me to follow. When I reached him at the bottom of the hill he was vomiting. I wondered why.

My rose-lit memory probably plays me tricks, but I remember no rain that summer and that I made an exquisite costume of a secondhand tank suit which I cut down to *here*, front and back, and edged with crochet stitches in pretty colors. The swimming was cool and fresh, as silky as flying into a cloudless sky; the meadow a carpet of tender flowers; the shapely rock walls were a large palette of subtle colors, almost ours alone. We were a faun and his naiad playing ancient measures, I liked to think, while our drunken old Bacchus pulled berries and vegetables out of his disordered, overflowing garden to feed us. The only disturbing notes came from a tent across the meadow, as big clattering masculine laughter and shrill female scolding. We met the couple—tall, raw young Marty and his tiny sharp-faced girl friend, Marie—at the quarry a few times and one evening went to visit their tent: they were having a party, why didn't we come? The beds had been taken out of the tent and the table and benches laden with bottles of liquor and bowls of peanuts and popcorn. There were no introductions; we simply milled around together and danced to the raucous music of an old phonograph. When the mass became individuals, I noticed a short, fat young man following Marty around with a fixed, adoring smile. Every now and then Marty put a tablet or powder (it was done quickly and I couldn't see precisely what the substance was) into Fatty's drink, absorbed in one long gulp. As the evening grew noisier and merrier, Marty called, "Stop, everybody. Fatty and I are going to do our trick." The phonograph was silenced. Marty brought in a chair and stood on it. "Now, Fatty, get in back of the chair and kneel down." Fatty staggered over and fell to his knees, as commanded, back of the chair. Marty then bent over from his height and between the rungs of the chair called softly, "Hey, Fatty, how do I look? Upside down? No. You're the one who's upside down. I'm upright." Fatty began to whimper and cry. "Don't do that, Marty. Please don't do that. Don't mix me up. Don't be upside down. Don't make me upside down. Please." The whimper became shrieks: "Take me out, take me out of this cage. Make me straight. Take your crazy upside-down head away. I'll die if you don't. Marty, you're my best friend, I love you. Please, please, get me out of here." It was tiny Marie who pulled Fatty away and pushed him, stumbling, shivering, out of the tent. I started out too, furious with all of them. Davy immediately followed, asking what I was so upset about. Angry with him too, I shouted that using Fatty for his cruel act, doping him to perform it, made Marty—witty, imaginative, and maybe even a pretty good poet—a vicious beast.

Davy, who admired and probably envied Marty's swaggering, defiant life, couldn't understand why I thought him beyond contempt and yet accepted Guido and his goat without criticism. I wasn't quite sure, but in the course of several conversations we decided that it was a question of who victimized whom and the ensuing destructions. Guido's goat was well cared for, well fed, and, in several senses, well loved. She showed no ill effects from Guido's repetitions of the relief and pleasures he had known as a boy left alone for days to wander with grazing animals in frightening emptinesses of land. Marty, a so-called evolved man, was using his superior intelligence to make a beast of a frail being, to make, by persuasion, drugs, and the creature's own debilities, a nonperson, a slave, of Fatty. *"Es is doch a mench"* (Yet he is a human being), my mother's clarion call when my father reviled wops, micks, and niggers, rang in my ears; it was her short hymn to the wonderful uniqueness of human life, an expression of the respect, to the degree of religious awe, every person owed his fellow man. This emotion which was also her law settled deeply in her children and, as repeated to Davy, explained to him why I found Marty so loathsome. Though at least partially understanding my reaction, Davy remained fascinated by the high life in the tent across the meadow and visited a couple of times without me.

A couple of weeks after we had settled in, I telephoned my mother from the Bergsons' and invited her to come one Sunday, to rest and breathe some fresh air after a hard week's work. (We had, gradually, cautiously, become quite friendly.) She arrived in the car she had recently bought and which my father drove; she had, she said, no interest in or talent for such sophisticated machinery as autos; only sewing machines. She descended from her car as aristocratically and languidly as her short, plump body would allow and, having greeted us, looked around with pleasure at our trees and our wildflowers. She wanted to put her toes in the quarry and meet the old Italian who loved a goat. Did he? *Really?* She was as curious about this new mode of love as she had been about homosexuality when my brother and I enlightened her and when, with sudden recognition, she remembered a woman in Warsaw who dressed like a man and kept another woman as a kind of wife. My father said "Pheh!" and stayed silent. The irregularity of our situation, Davy's and mine, was beyond his capacity to understand and difficult to endure. He had already interfered with my most innocent dates, like going to an afternoon movie with a boy; he had dragged me away from groups that included boys; he followed me when he suspected I was following or, more exactly, spying on a popular boy on whom I had a despairing crush. Here, now, sat his crazy wife beaming at the *shmendrick* Davy and street girl me, living "free love" like wild anarchists. He couldn't protest much, however. The car was hers, the new carpet for the living room was paid for by the earnings of the corset shop she had finally achieved after years of door-to-door selling. She could now afford two skilled helpers and a Persian lamb fur coat and the diamond ring she never before owned. She had already told him, I found out later, that if he didn't like life with her, he was welcome to try it without her, but she never told him flatly to leave. She didn't want the aloneness, nor the sexlessness, nor the absence of light quarreling; they still argued, in a desultory way, out of habit. He hung on, also, because he liked to watch the ringing cash register in the store when he was not on his job. He enjoyed checking inventory and would go down to lower Broadway on Sundays to buy replacements of corset material, bones, hooks, and ready-made girdles and bras, swaggering, ordering people about, being the entrepreneur he wasn't. He had his uses, she conceded, including driving the car which gave her a great freedom she never had before. It was, like their domestic life generally as they grew older, a fairly good symbiotic arrangement.

After the exploration of our Elysian Fields and a view of the quarry and the wide country sky, she proceeded to lift out of the car a heap of grocery boxes. He never helped. It was his form of protest, and anyhow, no self-respecting man ever carried so much as a small paper bag of groceries, no matter how desperate the need. The grocer's cartons spilled and kept spilling gorgeous things, food for at least a week: bagels, eggs, cans of salmon, sardines, and tuna fish, big lumps of cheese, canned soups, two roasted chickens, cakes like palaces, only half of which we could cram into our small cupboard and icebox. (I can't remember where we got the ice, unless our landlord supplied it; he performed a surprising number of services when he shone with wine and love.) One of the ornaments of the prodigious Sunday meals we consumed was the abominable cheese-cement turnovers my mother made every Friday and with great pleasure. These, she felt, contradicted her reputation for being a lousy cook. (They didn't; rather, fortified it.) For dessert, also, a bounty of fruit with an injunction to Davy to eat, while I looked and looked before I reached. She rarely forgot to comment on the fact that since I had been a child I loved the colors and shapes of fruit almost more than I liked the taste. This one of my oddities pleased her; it indicated that I was artistic.

When we had absorbed as much of the fruit and the home-made little monsters as we could, we stretched our blankets out on the grass and talked. We told stories of our endlessly fascinating landlord, we talked of our few young neighbors and of the doings in the Bergsons' community on the other side of the highway—who was chasing whom in the fashionable games of changing partners, threatening to the older women and hard on the older men, too tired for the game. We talked about the corset store, and my mother, always a fine mimic and raconteur, told the week's story of Mrs. Greenberg, a frequent visitor though never a customer.

My father and the neighbors dismissed her as a "Bellevue case." My mother was sorry for her, while she was entertained by her costumes and her extravagant, dramatic monologues. She always made her welcome when Mrs. Greenberg chose to come into the shop, setting a chair for her as if she were a Romanoff grand duchess. The neighborhood scuttlebutt on Allerton Avenue, where my mother's shop was located, had it that Mrs. G. once owned a seven-room apartment on the Champs Élysées of the Bronx, the Grand Concourse, that she once had a *shvartzeh*—a black woman—to do her housework, her laundry, and cooking every day all day, that she had had a beaver coat and one of karakul and a fox cape, long. She once had, they said, two automobiles and a chauffeur and two long ropes of real pearls with earrings to match. Mrs. Greenberg was the stuff of legend until her husband took her furs and jewels and, leaving her without a cent, ran off with a singer of the Bronx Opera House. Where he had gone she never knew, nor did the police take much trouble tracking him down; after all, he had run off with his own property. Her children? She never got along with her daughter, who married a Canadian sales-man—of what she couldn't remember—and never wrote her from Toronto, where she now lived. Her son, the lodestar of her life, had married a *shikse* who made fun of her accent and her worn, out-of-fashion Bergdorf Goodman clothing. He sent her money regularly, a miser's pittance, which just about paid for her room and board with Mrs. Heller, who poisoned her bitter life, threatening to throw her out if she played the radio early or late, or whatever Mrs. Heller decided was early or late, or if she hung her washed stockings in the bathroom or over a chair in her room, wetting the rug a few drops. And that shrew, that cholera, twisted out of her tenants double the money they should have paid for the Gehennas she rented them.

The few times I saw her sitting in my mother's shop she appeared sick and gaunt and of high dignity. In my habit of giving valid reality to people by identifying them with literary characters, I saw Mrs. Greenberg as Queen Hecuba, "the winter-frozen bee" of *The Trojan Women*. My mother's response was less literary and more lively as she recited to us, while my father napped on a cot under a tree, Mrs. Greenberg's latest soliloquy. Although it was a hot day, my mother began, Mrs. G. was wearing an old fur piece, rubbed down to a band of leather, except for the balding sharp fox head whose eyes gleamed malevolently off her chest. On her head, a broken garden-party hat of pink straw with two daisies dripping off the brim (my mother's eyes, like her ears, rarely missed a detail); on her feet, the shapeless sandals she had ordered many years before in Greenwich Village so she could look like Mary Wigman, in one of her early flights of artistic aspiration. The loose, ragged, peplumed dress my mother described was probably of the same vintage, of the same dream. Having settled herself in the chair my mother placed for her and refused a cup of tea—she never accepted anything—she slowly perused row on row, shelf on shelf, all the boxes in the shop, then studied the three sewing machines and the women, including my mother, who made them whir and speed. After the unhurried studies, she rose. Walking to the center of the shop, imperiously pushing aside a customer who was in her way, she proclaimed in a rusty, cawing voice, one long arthritic finger pointing at the shelves and piles of boxes, "In all those boxes, those hundreds of boxes, what do you say is in them? You say it's laces and corset cloth, fancy brassieres, big surgical girdles with straps to hold tired *kishkas* [entrails] together, fake titties to put in bathing suits to fool men who think they're seeing the real thing. Those boxes could even be stuffed with money and diamonds and sables; your store could be bigger than Macy's and you could live in a palace on Fifth Avenue like a Rockefeller, you could have a dozen maids —white, Irishers—to serve you imported lox and keep a dress-maker who works only for you. But if you haven't got your health, ladies, or children who love you—never mind love: children who care whether you die or live—in those boxes, in all the boxes and in the palaces, is shit, only shit, nothing but shit. Believe me, I know." She turned, pushed the drooping daisies of her hat away from her eyes, and stalked out. Like a proud old cat, my mother said.

Gossip and annals exchanged, the chicken bones and orange peel gathered and wrapped, dusk coming on, my mother summoned my father and they drove off, she completely contented with her Sunday and us, he still dour and disapproving but not free to express it. Davy, though a *shmendrick*, was a good boy, a smart college boy who might be a doctor someday, or a lawyer; anyhow, someone who didn't work in a factory. As for me, I was so completely out of my father's control that although he continued to mutter, he no longer complained clearly or loudly about me, or at least not in my hearing, since our encounters were few.

On several Sundays they brought with them my little sister, at the time about nine years old and very happy to pick flowers and splash around the edge of the quarry. I noticed with some interest how solicitous my mother was of her, more like the nervous Jewish mothers of my childhood. She was tensely watchful that the child didn't go too far into the water, that she didn't shiver with cold; wrapped her in towels, rubbed her, and made her put on a fresh, dry dress, not hang around until the sun dried her, as we did. When I asked my mother about this special solicitude during one of the quiet autumnal afternoons we occasionally spent together, she said it was because my sister had been a sickly child—did I remember that she had to be fed bacon, of all things, on the doctor's orders?—who had anal pinworms and was very sick, with a high fever, with each tooth she cut. Surely I remembered the weeks we ran wild in Coney Island because she needed so much attention? Mostly, she said, it was guilt that made her so attentive. This one she didn't want, really didn't, especially since my brother and I were quite grown, six and a half and eight, when she became pregnant, and old enough to care for ourselves while she took on longer hours of work. And here this pregnancy, her fourteenth, and Dr. James (a New England aristocrat whose mission, now that he was retired from ordinary practice, was to perform abortions for immigrant women at no fee or little) would not, to her amazed disappointment, perform another abortion on her. He tried to help women, he had said sourly, not kill them. She was stuck, she didn't want this baby, not at all, not for a moment. Did I remember how tired she was, and how easily she cried? Now, of course, she loved the child, had loved her from birth, such a pretty and frail baby, but she never could forget the terrible feeling of not wanting her and begging Dr. James to change his mind, to try just one more abortion. For that she would feel forever guilty and, afraid that the little girl might in some way sense that early unwantedness, was especially indulgent and affectionate with her. And it was so nice to indulge her now that there was the corset store and money to spend on her, not like having had to be so stingy with us.

I once made a rough count of thirteen abortions between the time we came to America, when I was not quite five, and the time of my sister's birth; it came to about four abortions a year. My mother must have picked up some birth control information after my sister's birth, probably had learned about condoms and insisted my father use them. That there was some diminution in their sex lives after my mother's first, early heart attack I discovered when I found her giggling as she opened her door for me. She was amused because her doctor had told her that there was to be sex no more than twice a week, and she was anticipating the look on my father's face when she told him the black news. It has since occurred to me that a woman who had undergone so many abortions would have shrunk from or even cut off all sexual contact. Although it was dictated by her tradition and those of her friends and neighbors that she acquiesce to "men's needs," there were yet thousands on thousands of women who found some way out, headaches to hysterics. Since she resorted to none of the dodges, it would seem that my mother enjoyed sex and was fatalistic and stalwart about abortions, among women's common ordeals, and infinitely grateful that there was the old Yankee crane Dr. James to perform them. In my still naive years I sometimes wondered that my mother could tolerate men at all. She clearly could, playfully and delicately flirtatious (learned from the showgirl customers in her corset shop in Warsaw?) in her encounters with the husbands of her customers, many of them Italian and, in their peasant way, courteously responsive.

One of the injunctions of her doctor insisted that she walk a certain distance every fair day and she did, to Bronx Park, not far away, where she could rest on a bench before she returned. Shortly after the walks began I heard about Mr. Giordano, a retired butcher who also had heart disease, who also had to take walks. He was a nice gentleman, she said, who once in a while brought her cannoli and sfogliatelli, delectable Neapolitan cakes they shouldn't have eaten, but who could live on cottage cheese and lettuce all the time, so what the hell. They talked about their children, about his dead wife, Rosa, about how boring it was to be retired (she wasn't, and continued working until her death), about the flowers and trees around them and the garden he was planting for his grandchildren. I asked her if she ever met him outside the park, in a room, in his house maybe. She laughed and said, "I think we might if we could. But we're both broken crocks and what a terrible joke it would be if we killed each other in his bed, maybe under a picture of the Virgin Mary, like many Italian bedrooms have. No, we just walk and talk and that has to be enough." She would add wistfully, "Sometimes it feels like a lot. I haven't had such nice talking with a man for a long time." My mother died with an Italian text in her bed. The family story is that she was studying Italian to be able to speak with immigrant customers, to ascertain where there might be excessive pressure of steel or bone, to understand where straps on surgical girdles compressed the flesh painfully. That was quite true, but I never relinquished the thought that she might also have been learning Italian to flatter and please Mr. Giordano, to suggest a light shadow of being in love—my bit of spangle sewn on her short, narrow life.

She was still quite well, however, at the crest of her might and merriment, that quarry summer, tottering on her small high-heeled shoes as she scrambled, held on either side by myself and Davy, down the loose-stoned path to the quarry. She never went swimming; she didn't think short, fat women like herself should appear in bathing suits; it was ugly. She dabbled her feet in the water and kept a ceaselessly vigilant eye on my sister while Davy, holding her firmly, taught the child to swim. Shoes and stockings on again, Mama permitted us to pull her up the hill, laughing all the way. At the top, near the car, enclosed in his fief walled by the newspaper, sat my immobile father.

After the ceremonial "piece fruit" which marked the beginning or end of Jewish conversations, my mother announced,
one day, "I have an idea. Why should we keep the baby"—so
my sister was referred to until she went to college—"in the hot
city? I can't leave the store to take her away and it would be, if I
could do it, only for a week, no more. Her best friends are away
in the Catskill Mountains or Far Rockaway, or someplace, and
the poor thing wanders around and doesn't know what to do
with herself. So she stays alone in the house and reads too much.
So—why don't I bring her up here, to you? Of course I would
pay her board and give you a salary as mother's helpers."

That is how we teen-agers became the parents of a nine-year-
old and earned enough to keep ourselves comfortably at the
quarry for the rest of the summer and something left over for a
new pair of shoes and a heavy sweater in the fall. My sister,
always a winning child, was developing a pretty little wit; she
was a speaker of odd, arresting phrases and a maker of tunes
which she sang in a true, limpid voice. We taught her other
songs, which she learned with talented ease, and thus we spent
many evenings singing blues, cowboy songs, spirituals (which I
had learned on my visits with Joe to the Hall Johnson Choir in
Harlem), the old Irving Berlin songs—"All Alone," "Remember"—of my childhood, songs we had learned in school,
and snatches of Jewish chants we half knew, into the night. We
sang with a few neighbors at times, but most often as a trio, in
praise of the moon and the march of stars across the dappled
sky. We took her with us to the settlement across the highway,
leaving her with friends who had children her age. She enjoyed
the visits but was just as pleased to leave when we began the trek
back to our summer estate, completely contented to swim, to
pick blackberries, to stroke the family goat when Guido let her,
to be with us constantly, parted from us only by the India-print
curtain which separated our cots at night.

Her presence was, in spite of the curtain and her deep child's
sleep, an inhibitor and a welcome one. We had, with our small

knowledges and lack of experience, with Davy's fear of hurting me and my inability to encourage him—to reassure him that the pain of tearing through a hymen was not great and that I wouldn't mind—reached a discouraged state. It was easier to avoid sex than to admit that the best we could do was stroke each other, penetration avoided. Another inhibitor was the large, dark shadow of pregnancy. Davy had learned the names of condoms and knew the pharmacies that sold them. He had also learned that there were tears and holes in them sometimes, that semen could seep through dried-out "rubbers." He rejected the condoms, it seemed to me, also because they solved nothing about forcing a hymen, which he had begun to think of as an impenetrable wall. I had heard of thick, rigid hymens and maybe mine was like those. We couldn't afford to consult a physician—and what kind?—nor were there hospital clinics to help us, and there were no adults we could turn to for advice. I might have asked my mother, but I didn't know how to open the subject, nor could I easily confess failure of any kind to her. I needed the stance of knowing what I was doing at all times in order not to crumble. As the self-conscious cage of failure imprisoned us both, the affectionate and gratifying stroking stopped although we stayed close, devoted friends, pleased with each other's company and lonely without it. We never actually discussed it, but we must both have felt that sex that was too much like "feeling up" and had gone on too long was immature, inadequate, and we were profoundly ashamed not to be capable of the full adult act.

In spite of the embarrassed, frozen nights, the days were garlands of pleasure. Had we found the courage—Davy less frightened, I more thoughtful—to deflower me (a curious old euphemism, less graphic than the later "breaking the cherry"), I might now be Mrs. Davy or, as things go, the former Mrs. Davy. In a sneaky, subterranean way, I was preparing myself for the full, grown-up experience, with someone else if necessary, possibly a less talkative and younger Jones. I was determined that it would happen, not so much out of sexual hunger as from the need to know what the experience held, not to be ignorant, not to be left out. Ultimately what had to happen happened, but not for a while.

10. SIBLINGS REFOUND

Summer, as summers faithlessly do, left and we said good-bye to Guido, presenting him with a strongly odoriferous Italian salami as a farewell gift, patting La Bella's back affectionately, a farewell, as it were, to an old friend. In exchange he gave us a bottle of his cutthroat wine and, for my sister, a bagful of narcissus bulbs and instructions about how to nurture them. That fall we lined up enough jobs among our several semiskills to pay the rent on a one-room street-floor apartment near Fourteenth Street and the First Avenue market. The furnishings were a couch that opened into a bed, a bridge table that could hide in our one closet, two chairs, a two-burner stove that sat on a small icebox, two rows of open shelves; beyond the kitchen space was a bathroom, its door studded with hooks for coats.

The bulbs on the wall in their paper caps were enchantments and so were our lumpy couch and my own stove and, on a shelf, two elderly pots, a frying pan my mother gave me, and a few dishes we bought in the market. I was enamored of it all and Davy swelled like an English squire as he counted out our money to pay the rent. We lived there for over a year, in our Paul and Virginia fashion, smitten with everything around us, with ourselves and each other. We loved the market and its big cans of burning flames that warmed winter nights and blazed

the faces of the vendors, making stunning chiaroscuro paintings. We loved the pastries sold us cheaply by the local Sicilian
baker because they were a bit smashed around the edges. We
learned to make good spaghetti sauce from the tomato lady in
the market and Swedish meatballs from a painter neighbor.
Surrounded with crusty chunks of Italian bread, these were the
culinary offerings we fed our friends, a number of them
teachers and neighbors older than we. They always seemed to
enjoy the food hugely, not that in itself it was remarkable but,
possibly, because it had as an ingredient the courage and contempt for convention of two young lovers: "Romeo and Juliet,"
insisted one of Davy's teachers, grayly, soddenly married.

But I didn't immutably feel like Juliet. I had no nurse to pet
or cosset me, no choice of princely suitors, no bejeweled
mother, no rich damasked father. I worked hard, running from
lessons to modeling to filing, to this job and to that, to do any
work that came my way, and just sufficiently attentive to school
to achieve, in time, the privileged English major. And I was
troubled, when I allowed myself to think about it, by my peculiar sex—or nonsex—life. No one, of course, knew of this, and
my heroine portrait painted in the Exchange at Hunter accrued
ever bolder colors. My independence had moved me into an
ultimate mastery of life: a real, full apartment in Manhattan, a
short walk from Greenwich Village, the haven of free love.
Some of my coterie became formally respectful, tongue-tied
when I addressed them. The loss of intimacy, the fading of the
earlier slapdash ease, bothered me very little. I hadn't much
time to hang around: too many jobs, a house to clean, I boasted
(actually quite casually and quickly done, since both Davy and I
were accustomed to the crowded disorder of not quite enough
closet space, too much bed in one small bedroom, heaps of
dishes in the sink, books piled on the floor). The very best of my
envied possessions was the full-time devoted boyfriend, who
more or less lived with me except when his straight-spoken
mother commanded that he stay at home; he was a member of
her family like his brothers and sisters until he was married, she

said, and he wasn't ready to get married yet, not by a long shot. Never mind his mother. To the girls we were a wondrous thing, princes of Eden and Xanadu, deserving of adulation and gifts. Millie brought a big curtain her mother had discarded for us to cover our discolored couch, Edith brought some forks, a knife, and a dish that her mother thought had been unkoshered by her careless son the "apostate," who used them for meat when they were meant for cheese, or some such mortal misdeed which I didn't follow while I happily accepted the gifts.

Our apartment added a new dimension to my brother's life. He had for some time called on me, in one room or another, to deliver the money my mother occasionally sent me. His habit had been to look around quickly and curiously, then take the money out of his pocket, hand it to me with a laconic "Here," and leave. Eleventh Street and its sociabilities made him slower, a lingerer. He had returned tall, muscled, and suntanned from a voyage to Cuba and back as a cabin boy. The trip had improved not only his looks but his manner and confidence; he had the cockiness to flirt attractively with college girls while he was still struggling through the infantilism of high school. His visits took place early in the evening, after school was over and he had finished his deliveries for the local drugstore. He had supper with Davy and myself and whatever friends hung around, friends reluctant to leave our charmed circle, reluctant to return to the Bronx or East Harlem, to half-crazy, unemployed fathers and testy mothers: "Where were you all this time? Downtown with your bum friends, their parents should be ashamed for allowing they should live together like that. Why don't they make them marry? What will they do when that crazy girl becomes pregnant? Who's going to keep her? With what?" And so endlessly on. Most often, the spur to go home finally was a paper unfinished. If the analysis of *The Winter's Tale* was submitted late, it was marked with a low grade, no matter what the quality. (The scares and woes of attending stern Hunter were many and the ultimate practical rewards limited. About the only jobs in fair supply were those in the welfare system then being established. Girls who might have been inventive physicists and inspiring teachers and critics, skillful translators in several languages, became and stayed throughout their lives—spinsters or married—social workers.)

Back to my brother: He loved all my friends—the young, the older, the short, the tall, the fat, the skinny—and at sixteen was not only an adroit flirt but an inspired dancer. And my friends were by no means immune to the "kid's" charms; they managed to make dates with him as they rode the subway together on their journeys home, and there was considerable gossip about the Baby Wonder in the Hunter Exchange. He didn't mind when I recounted it to his satisfied face.

My brother and I had stopped fighting for some time. Though we still argued, we had ceased battering each other's orbits. For long periods separated, we were no longer the classic siblings; were joined in a spiky friendship, rather. No longer each other's close concerns, both of us now challenged the world in different ways, with ever wider separate arenas to do battle in. I was free of responsibility for his dirty shirt and ripped knickers and he no longer had to obey when I screamed at him to stop playing stickball and come up to supper, right away.

The childhood wars over, I found myself mildly interested in him as something other than adversary, a hundred thorns in my life. First, he was droll, almost as droll as he was at two and rachitic, unable to walk but a cajoling, irrepressible talker and inventor of imaginative mischief. It was a revival of old nutty times to find him in the bathroom, during one of my visits to the Bronx, plucking at his armpits, trying to pull at a hair or two he thought he saw in the recalcitrant pink, smooth surface. Eventually they came, but he had a long, anxious time in front of the bathroom mirror, searching, pulling, willing the hairs to grow. On an invasion of the bathroom to catch him at yet another "How does my garden grow" search, I found him struggling with one of my discarded brassieres, which, since his back was considerably broader than mine, he couldn't close. I asked him if I could help. Rather than pull it off, surprised and embarrassed, as I expected, he muttered, "All right." After strenuous pulling, I managed to hook the bra and we both looked and laughed at the futile cups barely filled with unsuitable chest. "You won't make it," I said. "I don't want to. I wanted to know how it feels to be tightened all the time in a straitjacket like girls and other crazy people." "Oh, it's not so bad, no worse than having to shave every day"—a subject of some trouble to him at this time, since his cheeks were as slow as his armpits. "I suppose you're right," he said. "Shaving every day must be terrible. Movie actors probably have to shave two and even three times a day." My sophisticated response: "That's nothing. The worst thing is menstruating, feeling bad and angry and hateful for three or four days, then bleeding for about a week, with cramps and never knowing if you've stained your skirt and is everybody looking. And things like that." This usually led off, when we had the time for it, not running in several directions, to discussions of who suffered most, the shavers or the menstruators. In retrospect it seems a strange debate, which we kept going, with accretions of details and variations, for some time. We were educating each other and declaring a unity as maturing equals; no more big sister, no more little brother.

It was my mother who told me of an earlier stage in his sex education, long before he became obsessed with armpit hairs. She had given him permission to invite a dozen or so friends to celebrate their graduation from elementary school. My father was all for staying in the living room and seeing that the thirteen- and fourteen-year-olds behaved properly. My mother, having helped arrange the cream soda, the Baby Ruths, the cookies, and the chocolate kisses my brother bought out of his salary earned at the local drugstore, made vigorous efforts to get my father and herself out. She finally induced him to go to a movie, assuring him that these were good kids and would behave. If they really wanted to, they could get into trouble in the cellar or on the roof, or in someone else's apartment. "Come

on, you like Jeanette MacDonald." After the movie she took
him walking, he still eager to tear back to the house. Not yet,
she said, and asked that he buy her a hot chocolate. He wouldn't
walk anymore after she had finished. It was a cold night, he was
tired, he wanted to go home. There was no way to keep him out
after midnight, and they returned. The empty soda bottles
strewn all over and the candy wrappers clogging the kitchen
sink, the crumbs of cookies in the corners of the couch, didn't
disturb her; it was all to be expected. A glance into her bedroom
stopped her short. She called my brother to her. He appeared
with his hands full of cupcake papers meant for the garbage
pail, looking foolish and frightened. She said, "Take it easy, I'm
not going to do anything to you. You're too big a boy to punish
and I don't want to spoil your graduation. But just look at that
bed; there were bodies on it—you can tell by the crumbled
cover. I don't want to know who was on it or what they did."
Long pause, and then: "I just want to ask one thing: Do you
know that the girl has the baby, not the boy? Don't ever, ever
forget that." He was slow and quiet for days after, my mother
said.

My brother's curiosity and gossip about his drugstore clients,
the amusement they afforded him (several insisted on calling a
popular laxative, Feen-a-mint, "Shit Gum," he informed us
gleefully), and the scared faces of the boys older than himself
begging that he sell them condoms, appealed to his nascent
sense of power. For his affability, for his vast collection of arcane little facts (which kid wet the bed at twelve, which store was
selling bargain pants), for his links of knowledges and gossip
that made a tight and amusing village of the neighborhood, he
was called, as he strutted down the street swollen with inside
dope, "the Mayor of Allerton Avenue." Keeping my mother's
short, crisp bedroom lesson as a guiding rule, and as if he had
imbibed a certain primitive courtliness from that lesson, he
never in any way mistreated his girls, nor slighted them, except
when there were too many for one boy to juggle.

Not all the girls who ran at me for help, for influence with my brother, wanted adult sex; too scary. They wanted movie love, soft-eyed, surrounded by heart-shaped boxes of candy, a rose or two, walks in the park, and bashful light kissing under apple-blossom trees—a Lillian Gish–Charles Ray idyll. Though he tried to be considerate, the shyly romantic was not my brother's style, nor was he often inclined, in the promising excitements of variety, to concentrate on one girl. He seemed to like them all equally and prized himself in the courteous, playful pursuer role, like Robert Young, more than he prized the girls. It was one of my duties, when I visited my mother, to tell the tearful ones who haunted her apartment that he was never serious, that he would never attach himself to anyone, too footloose, and they were to find someone else. What was wrong with good-looking Benny around the corner, or that nice new boy, Tommy? So he *was* a *goy*. Her mother didn't have to know, and anyway she wasn't going to marry him. "Stop crying, it's making your nose red and swollen. Where's your handkerchief?" I liked the role of adviser to my brother's weepers, something like being a social worker or a teacher, more like the big sister I had been throughout my childhood, a role I thought I hated but apparently missed.

Besides being, as of old, but in a new light manner, my brother's keeper, I sometimes slipped into the surrogate-mother role of being my young sister's mentor, not always an unqualified success. We had gotten to know and like each other during our quarry summer and it was later reasonable that, when I had the time, I would take her shopping, introducing her to the charms of Klein's and Ohrbach's on Union Square. Here matters went smoothly, she trusting my judgment, voicing very little dissent. She became her own woman in the public library, where I tried to help her pick out books. After several visits in quiet acquiescence, she stopped me, protesting: "I don't want any more fairy tales, not the Green, not the Blue, not the Red, and no more books about Dutch Twins or Belgian Twins or Japanese Twins. I want to read harder books, about real people, about real girls like me, and please don't try to find them. I will, thank you." On my next visit she flourished a library copy of *My Ántonia* by Willa Cather at me.

We explored the Metropolitan Museum, where the naked ladies and gentlemen entranced her; she stood for a long time with the nude Greeks and an even longer time before the late Renaissance goddesses of Venice. Both she and I were smitten with the tawny supermasculine Etruscan warrior of the huge staring eyes who was later discarded as a fake; we wouldn't believe it except as a dreadful injustice. Because she had a pretty voice and learned quickly, I tried to sing Schubert songs with her, picking out the accompaniments on the piano in my mother's apartment, the piano I wouldn't touch years before. This was another occasion when I pushed too hard and failed; the German words baffled her and she would not sing that which was incomprehensible. We remained close friends, though; I too often putting on the old childhood mask of the guide, she as frequently, tactfully, rejecting my suggestions, until subtle changes made of me, at times, the younger sister and she the older and wiser. We exchanged these parts, a useful and happy arrangement, for the rest of our time together.

11. HIGH LIFE

One Christmas vacation promised to be a stinker. Davy had to go to Florida to help his uncle Moe, who paid him well to take care of the clients in his Miami boardinghouse. I had time for extra hours on jobs and for overdue class papers, and time to enjoy the smell of bundles of fir trees and their country green, staring meekly, like rows of prisoners, out of street lots. There was time to enjoy the shiny, brittle ornaments in Woolworth's and the glittering tinsel. The rest—the angels and lights, the beribboned boxes, the black Salvation Army pot, the interminable repetitions of "Silent Night" and "Jingle Bells," were, as our Jewish parents and grandparents said, "*Goyim naches,*" and who needed it? (We did, but couldn't say so.) Being alone in the apartment was uncomfortable, and besides, I was having landlord trouble. Our landlord, a pleasant man who called himself Garibaldi and wore a swooping, discolored hat to tighten the link with his hero, had informed me that though I was a nice, *bella* girl, he needed my downstairs apartment for his nephew Riccardo and his wife, who was far advanced in her first pregnancy and couldn't climb the five flights of stairs to their present apartment. Concetta got dizzy, she said, from the height and from dragging her big belly; she was afraid she would faint and fall and mash Riccardo junior. Also, she couldn't anymore go to the toilet in the hall. She didn't make it fast enough with the baby pressing so hard that she almost peed in her pants before she got there. And if there was another tenant in the hall toilet? She might die trying to hold it in, which she couldn't most of the time, or if she did, her bladder might break. A patient, inexhaustible nagger, she frightened Riccardo into nagging Garibaldi who nagged me to give her my ground-floor apartment and its private toilet. I had seen a good number of bellies in my childhood, worried about them, hated them, especially my mother's before it pushed my sister out and when I heard that I was pulled out with "instruments" that cut and tore at my mother. None of these images or fears attached themselves with any sympathy to Concetta, who could dree her own weird—a phrase picked up in my Anglo-Saxon class and vengefully useful.

I would go away. Garibaldi wouldn't put my stuff out into the street while I was gone; he was too nice and too lazy. I couldn't go with Davy, his uncle was paying his fare and certainly would not pay mine. He didn't like me much; none of Davy's family did except his sweet, slow father. After some thought, and dispelling a faint stickiness of distaste, I decided to accept an invitation that had been pressed on me for weeks.

One odd, unexpected time in the semester, a stranger, not of Hunter, had walked into my Shakespeare II class, sat herself under the professor's eye, opened her genuine leather notebook, extracted a gold-capped fountain pen from her alligator bag, and begun to make rapid notes. It became obvious, after a week or two, that her interest in Falstaff and the Richards was considerably less than her need to impress those around her. She had little success with the professor, whom she approached with questions, not always inane, at the end of class. A dry old scholar immortally in love with Portia and Ophelia, Beatrice and Viola, finding no facsimiles in any of us bundles of ungraceful flesh and no elegance of spirit, brushed off all questioners, muttering "Another class," and rushed out. A few of the girls the newcomer approached were apprehensive; she was

too ardent in her courtship. We didn't quite know what to make
of her. She was eight or ten years older than most of us and
spoke of having attended, for varying periods, Vassar, Oxford,
Bryn Mawr, and the Sorbonne, her schooling interrupted by a
mysterious ailment. (At this point of her stories we were taken
to Swiss sanatoria that closely suggested *The Magic Mountain*.)
Her coats were too expensive—one of real fur—she had too
many dresses, good ones, her shoes were made by an Italian
craftsman and looked it, her pocketbooks were cut of rare skins.
She was far too upper class for us, and furthermore, her body
and looks were disturbingly inappropriate to her glamorous
adventures and queenly belongings. She was short and ema-
ciated. Her brown hair crept down to a forehead of thick, matte
skin like blotting paper, almost to meet heavy masculine eyebrows. She did have compelling eyes, flat gray and large, the
blotting paper under them gathered around a thin mouth and
short chin—hardly a face at all except for the eyes. Some of us
found it repellent when she came very close and stuck her face
under our chins, looking up pleading and expectant as she tried
to seduce us with her gifts of an enchanted past and privileged
present.

She was a designer, she said, and liked to photograph her
models in the nude and then in the clothing she created for
them. Hunter? Oh, with only a year to go, she might get her
degree this time. Anyhow, she was going to be married soon.
Her father was one of the most prestigious lawyers in New
York, she said, and kept her in Hunter only because he wanted
her near home. (Why not Barnard, NYU? leapt simultaneously
and unspoken to our minds.) On the fee her father had earned
in a big case some years ago, he had bought a big house in
Brooklyn, probably designed by Stanford White, some experts
said. Why didn't we come to Brooklyn to see the house, really
unusual, have tea there, and meet her interesting father and
mother? A family legend had it that Mama was, when young,
the mistress of a Polish nobleman (each classic cheap-novel detail distanced us increasingly from her; she might have known it,

but couldn't stop). And we would love her dear, darling brother, who was a little sick right now—nothing much; he would be fine soon.

Rejected by the others, Sandra Rubinstein laid heavy siege to me. She had learned that I lived away from my parents and could go where I liked, and being more worldly and older than the rest, might not altogether disbelieve her stories of elite schools and worldwide travel. Between Davy's absence and Concetta's whining, she caught me at a weak moment and I agreed to go to her house for Christmas, to be photographed. The pay would be my keep plus a model's fee of ten dollars a day. So I packed some books and clothing, called my several employers to say I had to leave town for a while, and moved to Brooklyn for the holidays. The generous Middle European meals prepared by Sandra's mother and served on a well-dressed table were nectar compared to my usual meatballs and spaghetti or hot dogs with potato salad. Which fork to use for what course was a matter of watching the others; there was more difficulty in deciding how to handle the serving tools, how much to take off a large platter offered by the Negro maid. Sitting at the table as the brown arms slid toward me and away felt Hollywood and yet shameful, unnatural. The rich meat borscht and the stuffed cabbage, however, the homemade cheesecakes and nut cookies, soon dispelled the awkwardness of living beyond my habits.

The father, Mr. Rubinstein, was a slender man with a Phi Beta Kappa key on his chest and the high, shouting laugh of a fat man. Mama was good-looking in a ponderous way, never quite properly buttoned or arranged when she came to the table, having to be reminded that her dress had too much neckline, that her breasts were poking out of her brassiere. "Well, all right, all right, it's because I'm openhearted," and, laughing, she pulled the offending gaps to. She was preoccupied with several medical discoveries she had made, abetted by home medicine volumes she studied assiduously. Any pause in the conversation was ground for one of her discourses; a favorite:

"The cause of cancer is worriment and grief, too much worriment and grief." During my encounters with her I also learned that "Headaches is nervousness that runs from the body to the brain and makes mixtures that fight and hurt." Compared to my controlled, neatly dressed mother, she was a wilderness thing and aware of it, explaining her uninhibited speech and careless impromptu dress by the fact that she was born in Cossack country, where everyone was wild. She liked me only because I listened attentively to her psychosomatic revelations when no one else would. I liked her because of these eccentric enlightenments and her staccato, dramatic narratives. She would burst through the front door, trailing a Gypsy assortment of blouses, coats, and scarves, flowing, unbuttoned, her hand on her gasping, excited breast, spilling breathlessly, without a pause for hello: "Ay, did I just meet a lady, a friend of Mrs. Franks from across the street. She's so beautiful, with real blond hair and skin like white roses. She was wearing a stylish English tweed suit and a mink jacket and a string of pearls on her neck, real. I tell you, a beauty! She has her own millinery store and doesn't take any money from her *shlimazl* husband. Her children go to the Pestalozzi school and music camps. She speaks German and French, and her children, too. She wears a high-crowned silk hat she made herself; she looks gorgeous, like a czarina, like a queen, I tell you." Without a pause: "What am I saying? Pheh! There's nothing to her." I could never anticipate or understand the sudden paeans of praise and the swift falls, but waited for them and marveled.

For a few days Sandra and I were busy at photographic sessions, with intervals for good meals and Sandra's long telephone conversations. I found it all deeply absorbing: the once ambitious library of matched leather bindings that stopped with *War and Peace* and *Dombey and Son*, the variety of lounging robes dripping lengths of boa, worn by mother and daughter much of the day. To one who had never had a proper bathrobe, these were the gowns of princesses in grand palaces. But how to think of a Jewish family with a dog? The Rubinsteins were not obser-

vant, they ate shrimp and pork chops, but a *dog*? Dogs were for
Polish janitors and English lords in the red jackets of "Do ye ken
John Peel" sort of pictures. Jews didn't feed dogs—there were
too many hungry humans—and furthermore, dogs were malev-
olent assistants in pogroms. Many Jewish children of my genera-
tion were afraid of dogs, as I was, having been fed on indelible
stories. This one, however, was too cowardly and small and
pathetically ugly—bulging eyes, crooked teeth, and bowed
legs—to be anything but a caricature, and drooling constantly
at that. The women of the family adored and cosseted him, the
father loathed him and kicked him lightly, surreptitiously, when
the women weren't around. Then the terrified dog ran for
safety to the frail son, the one with the unidentified disease, who
hung around, more and more, during the clothed photograph-
ing sessions, making no comment, looking, looking. His silence
and pallor, his thick eyeglasses and the scarf wrapped around his
throat, made me back away from him as if he carried an unnamed plague. When the photography slacked off after a few
days, he invited me to a movie and proved more talkative than
in the presence of his family. His conversations—actually
monologues—on the walk to and from the movies were chillingly morbid, concerned mainly with monstrous births. Educated out of his mother's books and old medical volumes bought
secondhand, he was well informed and graphically detailed in
his information about spina bifida and hydrocephaly, even
stopping to sketch quickly, in the notebook he always carried,
the dreadful contours of these unhuman babies. When I begged
him to stop, threatening to walk away if he didn't—he became,
at times, more monstrous in his enthusiasm than his subjects—
he turned to music and the new recordings he had bought for
his extensive collection. He couldn't stay away, though, from his
prime obsession, "birth mistakes," and in the course of describing a Schnabel performance of a Beethoven sonata, suddenly
said, "Here's something interesting, not too morbid. Do you
know that some people's bodies have cysts that contain human
hair or a tooth? You know what that is? It's a twin that never

developed but became incorporated in the body of the baby that did. Sometimes—and this is even more interesting—they take a baby out and find a kind of extra skin sticking to it. The skin has the full form of another baby. The healthy cannibal sucks it dry, blood, bones, and all, to feed itself." It was impossible not to think that somewhere, he felt, a twin had half consumed him, that he was a feeble, emptied envelope, and that with study and observation he could remedy his situation, become strong again, or at least resigned to his anomalous state.

I consented to go to the movies again with him only after he promised not to talk about birth defects. He didn't, but bought me a soda and expensive English mints to eat during the show. In the following days, he became more courtly and flattering, his apogee of praise the mumbled statement that I reminded him of the Spring Song of Siegfried's meeting with Sieglinde. (Not until I became a mild Wagnerite did I appreciate the warmth of the compliment.) Papa presented me with a bunch of flowers—"Sweets to the sweet," and he guffawed in his fat man's bellow. Mama consulted me about dinner—would I like veal chops with sour cream or chicken in lemon sauce? I was introduced to relatives and distinguished friends, among them a leading obstetrician of Brooklyn, whose spring and summer costume, he boasted, was an outfit for golfing, including clubs, to impress his patients with the fact that he tore off some fictitious golf course or other to be immediately with them in their painful need. When I sneezed, there was quick solicitude from Mama and Papa—was I catching a cold, God forbid? How pretty and unusual I looked in my earrings. How smart I must be in school with such an intelligent face; surely I would make Phi Beta Kappa.

Sandra brought me little presents—a wallet, a scarf—and the family presents came faster and faster, increasingly expensive, as if to display the delights I would enjoy as a member of this prosperous, generous family. They were crowding me, urging me to love them and Sam, who needed a strong, healthy girl. I didn't want to live here, to be part of them and under their control. I had been invited for work and that was all. Though only several days of the holiday were gone, the sickly sweet praise, the forced attention, Sam's mania becoming heavily oppressive, Mama's medical inventions no longer amusing, I wanted to go back to Eleventh Street to brave Garibaldi and Concetta's belly. But the bed and board in Brooklyn were sybaritic and the promised salary munificent as compared to the wages I received for much rougher work in my screaming laundry. I stayed; waiting, wary, preparing for some sort of overt proposition that would probably first come from wild Cossack Mama in her stained blue velvet dressing gown with the stringy boa.

It came one evening over the nuts and fruit on the round dining table. Mama led off, asking if I liked Sammy, her son. Ready as I was, I still found the question annoying and hated them all. I said I liked him but not very especially. Papa clattered his loud laugh—how cute I looked blushing—and pushed Sam's hand nearer mine as they lay on the table. Sam grew uneasy and dropped his hands in his lap. Mama went on: Sandra was going to be married soon—she supposed I knew—to a successful young accountant, Rick, but unfortunately she couldn't have children: her bones were too narrow and her health too frail, the doctor had said. So, Mama went on reasonably, why shouldn't I marry Sam, whose sickness would be over in a short time, he only needed some rest. We might marry in the late spring. I liked children, didn't I? I had spoken so affectionately about the kids I baby-sat. Such a fresh, young, healthy girl like me could have lots of babies. So-o-o—a sententious pause—my first would go to Sandra and Rick because they were older, the next I could keep for myself and Sam; the third would be theirs, the fourth ours, and so on.

Since I had left my parents' house to live with others—as mother's helper, as companion, as tenant, as tutor—I had learned to anticipate strikes of madness, when ordinary rooms become crooked, surrealistic, when smiles were suddenly carnivorous, issuing from frightening maws. I had also learned control and an accompanying degree of politeness. Instead of flaring up as my head and limbs urged me to, screaming "How can you—Jews—talk about giving and taking babies, like dirty, thieving Gypsies? You're not only crazy, you're immoral!" I laughed a little, not too difficult since somewhere in my anger was a strand of amusement over these madmen. "What makes you think I'm a baby machine? How do you know I want children and how soon I want them if at all? When I came here it was on hire, only for modeling, not as a permanent purchase of a one-woman obstetrics ward. Good night, I'm leaving tomorrow morning." Sandra ran after me to the spare room I used, a place of boxes and chests of drawers and a decent bed attached to a small bathroom. She pleaded with me not to leave, wouldn't I please, please stay until the end of the vacation, when she would give me all my money, one hundred dollars. It would be terrible to break into her project, which was going so well. I agreed to stay after she swore to get her family off my neck; no more talk of marriage or babies.

I couldn't find her the next morning, and leaving a message with the maid that I would be back in a day or two, took myself off for a short break of movies, pastrami sandwiches, and comfortable friendships. When I phoned the Rubinstein house the next day, I was told that Sandra had flown off to visit friends in Atlanta and would be back in a couple of days. Back to my footloose friends. When we ran out of movie money we walked and walked, exploring Hester and Essex streets, streets of Greek stables, of huge round cheeses and long, fat logs of Italian sausages, the dim sinister alleys that hung off Canal Street toward Chinatown, vowing there that some moneyed day we would feast of the myriad dumplings that misted and perfumed the air of Doyers Street.

The night of my return, Sandra still absent, the Rubinsteins had a party whose star attraction was an animated, coquettish woman who played small roles in the Yiddish theater. Her effects were good: bobbing, burbling under auburn curls like Shirley Temple at one moment; sloe-eyed long looks under

drooping lids and a muted drawl the next minute. Another
design was to be mysteriously silent for a while and then, pointing herself at a male target, to bombard the speechless object
with eloquent high praise. Early in the evening there was no one
to engulf: Papa knew her too well and laughed, Sam was afraid
of her and despised her, Rick, Sandra's fiancé, whom I hadn't
yet met, was working late and would arrive after dinner.

While the dessert was being served, a stocky young man with
a high complexion burst into the dining room, a telegram shaking in his right hand. "What's the matter, Rick?" came from
several directions. "I'll tell you what's the matter. This telegram
came from your darling daughter Sandra. She's having such a
good time with her friends, and I suppose their brothers in their
white linen suits and their mason jars of moonshine, that she
thinks she'll stay a little while longer. What kind of while? For
going to bed with all of them? And come back to me with Dixie
gonorrhea?" Turning to Mr. Rubinstein: "You can phone her
and tell her to stay on and on. She won't find me around when
she gets back." Mama and Papa ran to him, patted his hands,
caressed his cheeks, stroked his back, begging him not to be
impulsive. He knew how mischievous Sandra could be; she was
only playing games with him, trying to make him jealous, that's
all. A sophisticated man like Rick should understand a silly
female impulse that meant nothing but a bid for extra attention.

Into the excited huddle came our minor Molly Picon, Francie, who took his manicured, ruby-ringed hand and led him into
the living room, the salon of red plush drapes and chairs, the
blue Oriental rug, the Steinway grand, the inlaid Chinese tables
and the glass cabinet of chinoiserie, a room for serious discussion, or seduction. Francie chose her surest field. Settling herself close to him on the velvet couch, she lifted Rick's hand and,
looking around saucily, said, "Has anyone seen before such an
aristocratic hand, a thinker's hand, an artist's hand? And look at
that profile"—turning his chin cradled in her red-tinted
fingers—"just look at that profile; it's much better than John
Barrymore's. And the full face is more sex-appealing than that

drunkard's. There's Italian heat in those deep brown eyes. Your grandmother was Sicilian, a passionate Sicilian beauty, wasn't she, Valentino?" Her elderly husband was snoring softly in a dim corner of the room, the Rubinsteins weren't enjoying the seduction, they were too worried, and I soon had enough of the foolishness of the whole scene, including Rick's descent into calm, then purring pleasure and a taut crotch. I went upstairs to the library to read. But Francie's sinuous voice kept sliding over the pages. She was now shamelessly extolling Rick's charming personality, his acumen as a businessman, his generosity to his parents and grandparents.

Her voice faded away into last good nights at about midnight, and the snap of the safety lock on the front door. Rick came up the stairs and stood before me, close. He was drunk and intensely agitated, feral and threatening, looming over me like a great buck ready to dig his horns into me. Anger, liquor, and sensual stroking words had set him trembling in a menacing ecstasy. I slid away from under him and dashed to the bathroom, where I stayed until I thought he had gone into Sandra's room and to bed. I found him standing at a window of the library staring out at the garage, far back in the yard. "Come here," he said. I obeyed. Pointing at the boxes in the open upper story of the garage, he said, "Wanna see me shoot those boxes down, every one of them? That's more than a hundred yards away, isn't it?" I said nothing and still nothing when he pulled a small gun out of his pocket and began to aim at the boxes. "Please don't; they'll hear you and be scared." "No, they won't; there's a silencer on this gun." I, still trying to hold back time and threatening events, said, "How come you've got a gun? Isn't that illegal?" "No, sweetie, I have a permit. I got it through some friends." The veins stood out on his head, he became again the plunging, aggressive animal as he leaned out the window and shot, unfailingly, box after toppling box. I kept whispering, "Stop, please stop!" He kept on shooting, then suddenly turned, his gun pointing straight at me. "You saw what happened to those boxes. That'll happen to Sandra if I find out

that she's fucking those Atlanta boys. And if you say a word
about the gun—or anything—I'll shoot you, too. Maybe I'll
fuck you first." As I stood motionless with fear, he shot into the
books on the shelves above my head and into a sofa pillow near
my arm. Then he turned the gun in his hand, examining it
intimately, affectionately. He put it back in his pocket and
closed himself in the bathroom.

I slept fitfully, listening for the soft splat of his gun. Quite
different sounds came through my door at about four in the
morning. Opening the door a crack, I could see him standing
before the mirror of the open dressing alcove we shared, wearing only the bottoms of his blue silk pajamas. As he hummed
softly, contentedly, he tweezed hairs from his nose and from the
clumps in his armpits. He stroked his chest and followed the
slope of his sides to the curve of his ribs with satisfied fingers.
He opened the cord of his pajama trousers, dropped them to lift
his penis, and inspected it carefully with a look of approval. He
plucked a few pubic hairs with his tweezers, pulled up his pajama pants, and like a mother powdering a baby, he tenderly
patted talcum powder on his torso. He then turned out the light
and disappeared.

The next day was Saturday and I assumed that Rick, his
alcohol and self-love, would rest long that morning. Quite early
I went down to warn Mr. Rubinstein to get Sandra home
quickly and be prepared for Rick's gun when she did get back.
Mr. Rubinstein phoned Sandra, told her to be back the next
morning, Sunday, without excuses or delay. Then I took myself
off, books, clothing, and all, to Eleventh Street, safe from Mr.
Garibaldi, who spent his Saturdays playing boccie on Houston
Street. When we met in Manhattan the following Monday, Sandra told me with a proud smile that her father and his partner
had met her, holding Rick tightly by either arm. Impatient with
the story she was expanding in length and drama, I broke in to
tell her that I was no longer going to stay at her house and
would like the money I had already earned. School was going to
start in a few days and I needed the money and the time to catch

up on neglected school assignments. Sure, sure, she would give me the money, but she was a little pressed now with all that partying in Atlanta and the fare and presents to her hostess. She would have it soon, though. In the meantime, couldn't we take some of it out in entertainments, like paying for my admission and drinks in some famous Harlem speakeasy clubs, like Dickie Wells's and another that was owned by friends. I had begun to doubt that I would get the money and this suggested arrangement offered novel diversions, experiences that would make balls of fire as I told of them in the Hunter Exchange—not to Davy.

I learned a good deal more about Harlem with Sandra. If you were a regular patron, your waiter could buy you a reefer for fifty cents on almost any nearby corner. I learned that it was possible for a female entertainer to pick up a stiffly folded ten-dollar bill between her labia. It was a wow of an act, additionally rewarded by a bill tucked into the ribbons of a bra—money at the bottom and the top made a nice balance. The great climax of one show was the appearance of a man wearing a small contraption equally adept at the female money-eating trick. (My attempts at home with a crisp dollar bill and my own authentic equipment were dismal failures; it was a skill that required long practice, and were I to master the trick, where would I perform it? This would clearly not be one of my showpieces.)

Another delight of those evenings was the possibility of being picked up, for one drink or an evening of drinks, by a Broadway notable. One husky-voiced actress, enamored for the drunken moment of my storm of multi-yellow hair and what she called "Tibetan" cheekbones, invited me to sit with her for a drink. I accepted. She worked quickly, no time for subtleties, for the slow sensing of mutual rhythms. As I sipped my drink, she stroked my cheekbones for a moment or two and insisted I go home with her for the night. No longer awed or made shy by liquor-soaked luminaries, I answered (with too much icy poise, I suspect), "No, thanks." She spat "Bitch!" at me, roared at the waiter to take away my half-finished drink, and with her strong, agile behind pushed me off the bench we had been sharing. One night Sandra invited her brother Sam, who threatened to leave almost as we arrived; the waiter who helped him off with his coat had scrabbled at his anus while seemingly adjusting his jacket. We calmed Sam that night but not another, when we went to the apartment of two of Sandra's friends. In one of the dim rooms, bare except for large reproductions of the Belvedere Apollo and other soft Grecian youths, two young men were flicking at each other with light whips, gracefully, caressingly, giggling. Sam took off and I after him. Sandra stayed.

12. LIFE OF CRIME

As school and jobs again engulfed me, high life in Harlem closed its tantalizing, educational doors. I wrested no more than twenty-five dollars from Sandra; Concetta had her baby in her Aunt Rosa's house and moved next door to stay with her. Garibaldi and I became friends again.

The new semester offered promising explorations—the Cavalier poets, the Scottish Chaucerians, a second term of that Anglo-Saxon earl, Abraham, with his holdings of lands and ceorls, the now and then mystical mazes of Blake, the ornate mind and word games of Browning, and the sort of masturbatory verbal pleasures that were Swinburne's. I had a new Saturday job in Woolworth's, selling lipsticks, and a couple of my old ladies remained faithful in their English lessons. (I often wondered why they wanted to learn English, since their families addressed them in Russian or Polish or Yiddish. The answer when I questioned them did not betray so much intellectual ambition as avoidance of the dread word "greenhorn" and causing the daughters-in-law to think they understood every critical word spoken in English.)

In the dingy Exchange, a flatness of no new romances, no new slavish crushes; no one flunked out, no one threatened with Phi Beta Kappa possibilities, nor had the place been painted as promised. After I told my stories of life in a Stanford White house in Brooklyn and high adventure in Harlem, conversation settled into the mundane. The few excitements we could muster came from the classroom, where one of the habitual pleasures was to stump professors as nastily as we could. One of the science girls, a pre-med—if her father gave her the money for medical school, if she did well in chemistry and physics and biology, if medical school quotas limiting women would allow it—spent a fair amount of time positing and rehearsing the most effective puzzles with which to confront her biology teacher, the one who wore her Phi Beta Kappa key belligerently like a platelet of armor, on her high bosom. One day, during a lecture on the digestive system, Becky raised her hand and asked guilelessly why the stomach didn't digest itself. Let her answer that in front of the class, the Phi Betnik. The teacher fumbled and mumbled but had no answer. Later a few of us raised our voices in protest: "That's plagiarizing, it comes from Thomas Mann, he asked that question. You can't!" "Oh, can't I? Not in a million years would that illiterate read Thomas Mann. It's a very tiny chance and my stock may go up one thousand percent as an astute biologist, an original thinker, or maybe she'll just really hate me. I'll take the chance." In one variation or other, we bolder girls, most of us well-read, with the uncanny memories of youth, staged these little scenes, for fun, for wrapping the Olympians in discomfort. One linguist sharpie asked in class for a precise translation of an ambiguous line from the medieval French of the *Romance of the Rose*. The professor did not know or had forgotten. Palpably hating her questioner, she admitted defeat but was fair enough to credit the girl with meticulous scholarship, a victory for our side. I was interested, I told a Romantic poetry professor, in the life and works of Hartley Coleridge, the neglected son of the great Coleridge, who was for a while Wordsworth's charge. It seemed to me that he had had a brother who published his letters and poems. What was the brother's name and where might I find further references to him? The professor couldn't help me and didn't care to. To a lover of the pristine spirits of Shelley and Keats, the degenerate, drugged, and drunken Coleridges were beneath contempt, the detritus of literature. I lost that minor foray, without resentment, since I enjoyed this lissome, fawngloved, very minor poet-professor, who read to us weekly, as if it were religious litany, "La Belle Dame Sans Merci," with lovely shades of terror in his countertenor voice. (We didn't think he had to display his fear of women quite so blatantly while we admired wholeheartedly the infinite sadness he put into "The sedge is withered from the lake, And no birds sing!" These, he added, were among the greatest lines in all poetry. He convinced us and we stayed convinced.)

One mode of winning over professors was to be utterly, idiotically honest during a short-lived experiment that instituted an honor system like that enjoyed for many years by Virginia gentlemen in Jefferson's university at Charlottesville. It was announced in classes and halls that no proctors would be present at examinations; grown women, serious students, did not require monitoring. The gesture proved a shaming mistake. An indifferent mathematician hanging on to a C by short-bitten nails scored ninety-two on a trigonometry exam by copying from a gifted friend. A mediocre German student translated a subtle piece of Goethe amazingly well, helped by a prepared card lying in her lap, and earned an astonishing A-minus. Everyone became a wunderkind except myself.

I had requested a year of classical literature and philosophy instead of the alternative Latin, but for a forgotten reason I was forced into Latin, in which I had less than minimal interest. Read *Medea,* Plato, salacious Roman comedies—yes, heartily. But I was too disappointed and angry to study Latin and too much a snob to cheat. I would not copy from the baby whiz who knew all the rules of Latin grammar and apt examples for each, nor sequester bits of paper covered with Latin verbs in my bra or sleeve, nor allow myself to be distorted by a subject of which I knew, and was contented to know, nothing, nor diminish myself to follow the practices of hoi polloi, my frightened, competitive

Hunter friends. While the others were nervously rummaging for little papers inside their blouses or copying the papers of experts, I answered what I easily could and let the rest go, making the exam period short enough to allow for a couple of cigarettes in the Exchange before the next exam began. When the end of the term came, a few days later, I expected a failing grade; never mind, maybe then I would be allowed to register for the classics course. Grade cards were issued at the end of the last class; quite sure of an F on my card I found a C, a passing grade. "There must be some mistake; this can't be my card," I said to the young instructor. "It's your card, all right. Honesty should be given some reward. My respects and congratulations." (The honor system at Hunter was shortly dissolved, and never mentioned again.)

At about the time the teetery honor system was elevating Hunter's dignity, many Hunter girls were playing a simple, crooked game on Saturdays and the busy shopping days before Christmas in a popular department store. We English majors, companions of Beowulf, could rarely play the game; we were sequestered in a "rare"-book niche, where *The Last of the Mohicans, Little Women, Huckleberry Finn,* were sold in matched leatherette groups, ordered as "two feet of red with gilt lettering, no more than ten inches high"; room decorations, in short. Who could, if she wanted to, steal a green leatherette copy on thick paper of *Great Expectations?* Friends in other departments did much better: a pair of stockings, a fine handkerchief, a bracelet, could be slipped into stocking tops. But there were obvious dangerous limitations there; no matter how adroit, a girl might be observed by a store detective and arrested. The most profitable and safest Saturday game was for Hannah at the glove counter, for instance, to sell to Minna a pair of long opera gloves whose price was $16.50. Hannah accepted from Minna and rang up $1.25, the price of the cheapest gloves. Several days later Minna returned the opera gloves in the original wrapping and asked Hannah for a refund. Sorry, the gloves didn't fit her mother and since they were a gift she had discarded the sales slip. The fancy gloves went back into their drawer and Minna received $16.50, a handsome return for her expenditure of $1.25. Hannah was by far the best partner to work with. She was experienced and quick, having worked in several sorts of shops. Noticing her speed and poise, the personnel department made her a Saturday "floater," capable of learning speedily the goods and systems of any understaffed department. In order to know where and what she was selling, we arranged to meet with her at a given time in one particular toilet and began foraging—not in clumps, but discreetly one by one. Over several Saturdays, we bought bath sheets for the cost of washcloths, reclaiming the higher price on a later day. An ordinary syrup pitcher yielded the price of a costly vase, a cotton scarf brought proceeds from a Kashmiri shawl. Always the story was, "This was meant to be a gift, so I discarded the sales slip." We ate full lunches those weeks and bought extra pairs of stockings. Until store accountants began to study minutely discrepancies in slips and disbursements in several departments. The fat days were over, except for one last piece of mischief which earned no money. Nettie, who had never worked at anything before and inclined to easy agitation, was put by some malicious spirit into the toy department on the Saturday immediately before Christmas. She was deafened by questions, pummeled by children climbing up on her counter to pull down dolls and belled push toys. Their parents, sadists, she said, insisted on paying with checks, others with large bills for which she had no change; yet others presented her with long lists of purchases from various departments to which she was to add her own sale, with a special notation. There were foreigners whose requests she couldn't understand at all and always there were the agile, twelve-armed kids. Out of her mind with the confusions and her own helplessness, she quickly swept checks, slips, dolls, puzzles, wagons, musical tops, checker games, sales books, to the floor under her counter and fled, leaving a mess that might have cost the shop more than our assembled crookedness had.

Our thefts were often explained, particularly by those who were members or groupies of members of leftish youth groups, as small but telling skirmishes in the battle against capitalism. One skeptic countered with the fact that big shops lost huge sums to shoplifters but they were still flourishing, how come? Well, the idealogues with strong voices and convictions responded, thirty or forty bucks stolen from the capitalists would not make them fall, but we should at every opportunity, petty as it might seem, try to undermine them; thinking of them as the enemy to be victimized, no matter how, was proper practice for the revolution.

Sandra did not return to school for the spring semester and it was a relief not to have to listen to her autobiography begemmed with high living and multiple Don Juans. But I was still curious about her. Had she finally succeeded in making Rick so mad that he shot her? Were they getting married? Actually already married? On the excuse of asking for a misplaced book, I called Sandra's house. She was out, but I spoke to Mama, who knew nothing about a book, but why didn't I come for supper one night soon? "I bet you can use a good meal. I'm fixing calves' foot jelly and stuffed peppers for Thursday night. Come." I accepted, and arrived at about seven. The house looked startlingly beautiful. The rugs had been cleaned and their Oriental lozenges and paisley leaves shone like jewels; the small tables had been dazzlingly polished; the curtains hung white and stiff, flanked by the glowing red drapes. The shine, the smell, the color, appeared as intensely appealing as my mother's Friday night living room with the china closet glistening and the ceremonial tablecloth with the fat red roses spread on the round dining table. I was homesick, but life in the Bronx had been so prickly and unhandleable that I would not, could not, admit it and instead translated the homesickness into admiration of this house of strangers, another shade of longing. As I stood there dazzled by the beauties of the room, which I had once dismissed as overheavy, kitschy Middle European, it seemed that I *could* live here. I could marry Sam and have many babies to divide with Sandra. The family would take good care of me, feed and clothe me well, buy me rings and bracelets, and the maid would iron my blouses. I would finish Hunter and maybe the Rubinsteins would help me go on to graduate school between babies. It was an alluring picture for a girl often frightened and made lonely by her independence.

Tearing myself with reluctance from the seductions, I decided that life with the Rubinsteins was not really on my roster, their plump country was not for me. I visited rarely thereafter, and then not at all, my last picture that of Mama in one of her philosophical searches. One of the guests at a Friday night dinner was a young Chicago relative come to meet her fiancé's parents, who were New Yorkers. Mama: "Who is this boy you're going to marry?" "He's a boy I met at the University of Chicago. He's now studying law here in New York, at Columbia." "Can he support you?" "He will soon, when he graduates next year." "So then you'll get married?" "Of course." "Why of course?" "Because then we'll be happy." "So you'll be happy. And so what?"

The girl looked shattered, her security blanket taken from her. Mr. Rubinstein and Sam apologized for Mama—she doesn't often know what she's saying—and urged the girl to finish her dessert. She did, head down, troubled. Mama came clearer in my mind. Anyone who could say, "So you'll be happy. And so what?" had no measure for happiness or unhappiness— what did it matter?—nor concern for anyone's feelings, capable of taking babies and placing them where it suited her, if she was permitted. I said my farewells, forever farewells, to the Rubinsteins and returned to more innocent, less brutally cynical Hunter friends.

Birth control clinics existed, as witness the pessary of the foxy-faced girl, our infertility goddess, who offered it to anyone with a weekend date. The rest of us didn't know where the clinics were and didn't try to find them, much too afraid of potential trouble since we had heard that they were from time to time attacked by the law. Some of us took chances sexually because it was the brave, wiggling-finger-at-the-nose stance and because an abortion was an achievement of full, worldly womanhood. There were very few of us who used potential pregnancy to ensnare and marry our sexual partners. It would be an immoral act and, as a practicality, futile. Our boys worked at all sorts of odd jobs—as delivery boys, as shop clerks, as tutors, as movie ushers, as blood donors—in order not to burden their families while they attended college classes. Support a wife and child? Forget it, babe.

Most of our sexual encounters were truncated, gasping ventures made jumpy by the sound of a neighbor's step, an imagined turn of a key in a lock, or the cry of a child with whom one was baby-sitting. The semen spilled on stocking and underpants and inside trousers or, more awkward still, on trouser legs; kitchen rags and towels, hastily grabbed, carried off more semen than the girls did. Virgins were rarely deflowered under these circumstances, and knew an orgasm as an explosion set off by teasing touching and a warm spill of thick moisture on the thigh, the coitus interruptus method of birth control—a matter not so much of conscious control, however, as of inept haste. We knew only one girl who held the rope that led from pregnancy to marriage with a good-natured, acquiescent boy she had pursued, and raped, according to her friends. During the anxiety and turmoil of an unsuccessful search for abortion money, he married her. The marriage held up, as far as I know, maintained by her stubbornness and the forbearance that made him silent and bent-shouldered by the time he reached thirty— someone out of Yiddish folk tales of *shlemiels.* The rest of us played the field, not wildly, since there weren't enough candidates for dating in those hard-working, penniless days.

Whether I actually loved Davy or not, I am not quite sure. We loved our friendship and mutual admiration, we loved playing house and wandering the city together, we liked shopping in the market and cooking together; our united possessiveness and dependency made us feel large and strong. Bed was tender, considerate, sad, fumbling, and in time it faded into total discouragement. Davy would never consider infidelity with a more experienced woman, as a matter of romantic principle and probably because of his fear of failure. Back, not too far back, in my mind was a sureness that life with Davy was a beginning, a walking hand-in-hand in a spring garden of pink primroses and white daisies. In time, I knew, I would wander in darker copses with thorny bushes and strange flowers.

Experimenting once or twice, finally unvirgined—no great opening of the skies and no earth moving—I joined the worriers. Brave as we were, and as brightly, offhandedly *New Yorker*ish our manner when we mentioned it, our stomachs turned to burning knots as one week and a second and a third passed without a period. Money, money, money—where were we to get it? The fear of not finding money almost obliterated the fear of the operation itself. A decently performed abortion would be attended by a nurse who administered an anesthetic for a white-coated doctor in a brownstone on Irving Place or Stuyvesant Place. Appointments had to be made well in advance, and one departed in a taxi whose driver always knew when to raise a jump seat: "Put your legs up here, honey; I know you'll be most comfortable that way. I get a lot of girls like you around here." The cost? At least one hundred fifty dollars and more frequently two hundred. Appealing to parents for money even if they had it was hardly fruitful. A weeping, distraught mother: "*Gottenyu,* what happened to the nice girl you used to be? Who will marry you if you're not a virgin? Men can tell when a girl has had an abortion and some girls die from abortions." "No, Ma, people die of abortions only when they do it themselves with wire hangers and dirty scrapers and poison medicines. This is like going to a dentist's or a doctor's office, everything clean and careful, Ma. Don't cry, but see if you can find me some money, please." Only in extremis did one approach a father, who controlled the money. As my friends told it, the response ran: "Money for an abortion? Let the bum who knocked you up pay for it; he got the pleasure. Why don't you earn the money on the streets doing what you stupidly did for nothing? Even if I had the money to throw away, I wouldn't give it to you, you black plague." As in childhood, the less parents knew, the better. One's friends were more reliable.

I was hardly one of the dependable lenders since I had to pay my share of rent and food out of my earnings, but I could occasionally lend the five dollars my mother sent me now and then. Others lent what they could as the strangling days and weeks went by and the fear mounted that the safe period for an abortion would pass before the money was collected. Fears that sharpened with exam nerves—exams that required concentrated study of chemical formulae, exams that demanded precise recall of experiments in physics, exams that asked for long quotations from "The Parlement of Foules," all tortured times —should have helped serve as imperative warnings, but didn't. At almost any time a distraught friend would dash to our Exchange table, ashen faced: "I missed my period, it's two weeks already." "Maybe it's one of those irregular months." "No, I'm always regular and Joey said he thought his condom might have slipped. He saved fifty dollars and he's going to borrow twenty-five from his little brother's bar mitzvah loot—he told him that now that he was a man he had to help out with men's troubles —and his bachelor uncle, with his usual snide remarks and taking his own sweet time with stupid jokes and bathhouse wise-cracks, finally consented to lend him thirty. We need at least another fifty or maybe a hundred. How about you? You? You? Please, I'm going crazy and so is Joey." (It should be recorded that in my knowledge no City College boy ever denied his responsibility or removed himself from the money gathering. They were an honorable crew and were, somewhere under the fear, pleased with the knowledge that they were biologically ready to stop being "boys," ready to join or possibly displace their fathers as men.)

Though illegal, abortionists were not difficult to locate; everyone had a friend who had a friend who had an address and telephone number. And the address was not always Stuyvesant Square and its guild vicinity. Those who couldn't raise the larger sums could find a faceless room, a table, and a washbowl in Staten Island or the Bronx, or Jersey, no refinements assured or expected; price, one hundred dollars. My first was a New Jersey abortion, the result of drinking deeply of synthetic gin and romping with an anonymous beauty over house roofs and down some stairs or other, to roll on the grass in a nearby park. One effect of this minor Saturnalia was being transformed into a red shapeless thing, disfigured by poison ivy; the other was the pregnancy. My party hosts tracked down the young man; I hadn't wanted to because the fault was mine: I had designed the chase and led it off. He came through, though, with fifty dollars and I borrowed five dollars here, seven dollars there, another fifty, to pay for the arrangements made by an experienced friend's friend. My young man, no longer Adonis but a frightened pre-law student, borrowed a car and we drove out toward somewhere in Jersey, I too scrambled with fear to read the map and be of any help to him. After a couple of hours of driving onto highways and off, into rough and rougher roads, we came to a foursquare, unadorned stucco house standing alone in a field. When my feller rang the bell, a stout man in a creased shirt greeted us but didn't let us in until he had his hundred dollars in hand. He directed us to the back of the sparsely furnished house and indicated a chair for the boy to sit in and wait. I was taken to a kitchen with a large rectangular table in the center. The man told me to take my panties and stockings off and to get up on the table. There was no pad on the table, nothing but a wrinkled, coarse sheet and a shallow pillow which was removed as I climbed up. The man, whose face looked like soiled marzipan, said he was going to give me an anesthetic; lie still. I saw no needle, no vial of drugs, no mask, only a bulb syringe. This he inserted in me, letting loose a flood of icy water, the anesthetic whose effects lasted a few seconds. The man began to pull and cut at me, tearing, scraping, with a violence that threatened to rip out my intestines and stomach, everything in me to flood the table and floor and leave my body empty and dead. To remove myself from the pain I entered a delirious world of conjecture. How much pain must make mad-

ness? But maybe madness would go on and on as its own different, dreadful pain? But that, too, must ultimately end. In death.
But what if death were again endless pain? Around and around
I went, pain to madness with pain, to death with ceaseless, forever, pain. Until I felt the shock of another infusion of ice
water. The man pushed my legs to the floor, gave me two
sanitary pads, and said I could go, telling me to watch out for
the basin on the floor. I knew what was in the basin and, without
looking down, felt my way around it. As I stumbled to the door
the boy asked me how I was. I didn't answer. I didn't want to
talk to him. I had no connection with him except as a wavering
figure in a gin-washed dream I wanted to forget. He drove me
home, we murmured good night, and never met again.

My grand abortion was the result of an encounter with a
young poet, Arthur, whose techniques were erratic and uncertain, the girls told me, though he was fun—and for that reason I
felt safe. Confident in his lack of skill and underestimating my
receptivity (one of my friends said that a kind smile could make
me pregnant and I was rather proud of that; it equated me with
the great earth mothers of mythology—Demeter, Isis, and even
O'Neill's Nina), I missed a period and another. Arthur had
ninety dollars that he was saving for a flivver and I had forty
saved for a good warm coat. He managed to borrow some
money from a cousin and I from my mother, who was worried
but not censorious. After all, wasn't it she who had advocated a
life of lovers and had herself survived many abortions?

Like rich people, we bought the two-hundred-dollar abortion
on Irving Place. The room my friend Minna and I entered was
guarded by a nurse in white shoes, costume, and cap, the real
thing. She took my address and name (both false), age and
weight, and invited us to sit on a settee that already held two
women. We were all young, we in that room full of chairs and
couches and a table that held worn magazines, some of us twisting Woolworth wedding rings bought the day before. A few
girls picked up magazines, turned the pages quickly, and put
them down; a few girls held books whose pages didn't turn.

Mainly, we stared at each other's pale faces. There wasn't anything to say to Minna that I hadn't said before. I wanted nothing but to push two or three hours away, to be out of the room of the stricken girls and their whirling rings, of the idiotic prints that supremely insultingly featured women with babies—Japanese women with babies, French women with babies, Italian women with babies—laughing at us off the walls.

After about an hour of waiting, I was ushered into a room that looked satisfactorily surgical: a table draped in sheets of thick leatherette and towels, on movable, adjustable wheels. The doctor, a smooth young man in horn-rimmed glasses, introduced himself, assured me it would all be over swiftly and without pain. He then settled my head on a pillow, strapped my arms to my sides, and quickly placed a cone over my nose and mouth. He told me to count slowly to one hundred. I sank at sixty, sank completely and was gone, how long I don't know, until I felt someone stroke my cheek and kiss me on the mouth. I was dreaming; as reality this was impossible, insane. But I could hear his voice: "This is a pretty one. Come on, sweetheart, get up, it's all over, you'll be able to go home soon." He continued to kiss me, gently, then fervently, and slipped his hand under the sheet to my breast. A wave of wonder and rage woke me fully. I pushed his hand away. How could he? After mutilating my insides, how could he want to touch me? How could he? As I glared at him while he washed his hands and put his instruments into an autoclave, the nurse helped me off the table. She then accompanied me into a back room to rest on a cot among two or three other girls. Minna was still in the waiting room, I assumed, as I fell into a doze.

I was awakened by a rhythmic dripping sound. There were no sinks or toilets about that might make that sort of faucet sound. The dripping was close and it gradually occurred to me that I was the source. Lifting myself to look at the underside of my cot, I saw that it was spilling bright drops of blood, steadily, regularly. The window showed twilight, the girls on the other cots were gone. I was spiked by terror. Had everyone left—

nurses, patients, doctor, Minna—and forgotten about me? I got up and found towels to clean myself with and bleed into. Had they locked me in? Was there any way to get out? I walked through the rooms. No one in the operating room, no one in the small adjoining office. In the waiting room I found a cleaning woman, who gave me my panties and stockings and unlatched the street door. Minna was sitting on the stone stairs, sallow and looking elderly. She had been waiting all the long hours since noon and knew something terrible had happened, that I was too sick to be released, or worse still, that I had died. It was shockingly inhuman, she said, that no one had checked up on me. What if I had bled to death? What would they have done if they found me dead the next morning? They couldn't report a death in the ordinary way because the operations were illegal. Maybe they had a deep back garden for their burials or sold their dead late at night to medical students, who dragged them away to work on in hospital morgues. Maybe dead women were bound into sacks for highly bribed special sanitation men to pick up and dump surreptitiously with the rest of the city's garbage and filth. As Minna's imaginative indignation mounted and soared, I drooped in exhaustion, too tired to be angry.

The taxi, which was Minna's financial contribution to my abortion, took us back to her house, where she explained to her mother that I was having a small hemorrhage as the result of a polyp operation. Mrs. Speller looked skeptical but fed us a large dinner before I took the bus, still bleeding, back to my own apartment, to be comforted by the noises of my neighbors, the banging of crates and cellar doors as the market around the corner closed for its short night, pleased that Davy would spend that night in his parents' house. I thought again of what might have happened had I bled to death, how my corpse might have been disposed of, how Minna would spread the news of my death. I never once thought of the fetus—neither as an object nor as a potential baby. It was nothing, only a forbiddingly expensive nuisance, a thing that signaled passage into my mother's painful, gallant world.

POSTLUDE

In her *Human Condition,* Hannah Arendt, speaking of the end of adolescence, says that "in word and deed we insert ourselves in the human world and the insertion is like a second birth," a swift abstraction with a suggestion of volition and the rational. A fuller, more detailed picture of my own adolescence draws a long, erratic labor, alternately pulling away from and pushing toward a vague new condition, a faint goal reached with difficulty since the second birth dragged with it vestigial forms that were slowly, reluctantly discarded, a few leaving indestructible shreds and stubborn shadows.

As I look back at the labor of my rebirth in its wayward progress, there appear long, contemplative pauses for unaccustomed thoughts and new, firm decisions, clean of hesitancies and vacillations. To replace the hindrances of fat, I drove it off, and in congratulating myself on my new shape as reasonably acceptable and maybe even sexy, threw off the shabby old gray raincoat that had been "I" for a couple of years. (The Borsalino stayed, no longer a hat but a treasure of faded Renaissance gold and a witness to important times and events.) I lost completely the flapping nostrils that had been appointed the antennae of my sensitivity. Lipstick, rouge, and powder were not yet for me, a symbol of plain living and high thinking, it once seemed, and now a welcome form of vanity, a conviction that I didn't need Woolworth's help to enhance my charms. The deep contralto voice forced its way up to an ordinary nonoperatic level and the overcareful, actress speech contented itself with being a fair imitation of the teachers to whom I listened carefully when I was an immigrant child. In any case, I had acquired the wisdom, during my rebirth passage, to know that job interviews for full-time work after college would go badly if I was judged too odd, too affected, a prickly object among smooth office anonymities. The fast quips, like those of Dorothy Parker and Robert Benchley, that I had traded with friends in Hunter's basement lost their little stings and whips and ultimately died when I became fond of a girl who didn't hear well; it was cruel to ask her to strain and to try to lip-read the bright nonsense at which I had been so quick, a skill that no longer gave me pleasure since I saw it give pain.

Telling transitions sometimes came when the rebirth struggle left me skinless and unprotected, not quite ready for the new human world. In one night's meanderings I saw and felt like a woman standing in a doorway, howling at a running man, "Come back, please come back! I won't say it again! Please, please!" On the next corner a drunk with a battered face put out a shaking hand for a few coins. My hand shakes as I give him a couple of dimes. I bump into cripples and dwarfs and blank-faced idiots who look a little like me in this Walpurgisnacht engraving. Earlier I would have made this night an exercise for toothsome description with a touch of literary hyperbole to distance the experience. Now it hurt, as the unhappy children in the castle school had hurt. When I was a child it was constantly puzzling that when my brother punched me I felt the pain, but when I punched him I felt nothing. That was changed; skinless and all nerve endings, I was subject to a universe of punches. Newspaper stories of floods could drown me, earthquakes strangled my breath and buried me, forest fires burned off my hair and boiled my eyes. I was no longer immune, no longer the mythical, separate, and privileged entity I had tried to design. I was earthbound and vulnerable, like anyone and everyone else. The girl of the singular destiny melded with other young women, who tried to look like happy, bright birds as they fearfully approached job interviews, who had to search for places to live, enduring dank cellars and cold lofts when the money was low. My wide, fanciful travels in any corner of the globe I happened to choose would have to sink to hitchhiking, my intellectual entertainments among the cultivated elite would have to live in library books, in museums, in the movies, and in conversations with equally earthbound, unexotic friends. Now I could listen with patience and sympathy to their sorry tales of lousy bosses and thwarted loves, as I had found myself sympathizing with old Mrs. Sonntag in her loneliness, as I found myself heartsick and furious that I could do nothing to hold back my mother's decline.

I could only listen when my mother lightly complained about the endless cartons of dull cottage cheese she had to consume to keep her weight down, weight that burdened her prematurely worn-out heart. I could only listen as she spoke about aging as an overlong good-bye, like guests who stood and talked at the door long after one was ready to close it. Yet she was pining away for life as everything, she said, was going down, down, toward death; the breasts, the belly, the behind, even the front —you know where I mean—hang down like useless rags. Her slow, flat voice, once musical and lilting, kept intoning, "It's not nice to get old, it's not nice and there's nothing I can do about it." (I heard the same notes much later in a poet's sentence: "For the bleakness of December there is no solution.") My mother, who had once slept well and noisily, now slept little. Maybe she didn't want death to catch her unawares and preferred to take light catnaps in the back of her store with other people around who might—foolish, superstitious peasant idea, she said—warn her or hold death off altogether. It wasn't only that she couldn't do certain things; she had no wish or will to do them. Even if she could dance the mazurka without stopping her heart, would she want to now? There was the mandolin in the closet; she didn't want to play it, and—with a return of her gay laugh—there were those shiny dentures and she couldn't chew on a fresh, forbidden bagel with their strong, expensive whiteness. She hated the notion that they would still be shining and new, almost unused, when she died and that her new fur coat would still be new and the new rug hardly in need of cleaning. It was someone's idea of a joke, a terrible joke, that she should start dying when she could, finally, afford to start living.

There was nothing I could do with my pity. I could not relieve her anger and her fear, nor take the smallest part of them as my own burdens, a frustration as cruel as loss and death. When I began to leave her in the deepening twilights, plumping up yet another cushion, feeding her fish, watering her big rubber plant, reluctant to go except that I chose to avoid encounters with my father, who would shortly be returning from work, I, too, felt old and exhausted, angry and despairing. Almost, I was my mother and like her an intimate of death, no longer the invulnerable girl, responsible to no one and for no one.

The girl who was to be immortal, the bright fantasist and loony wanderer, was lost in the struggles of the second birthing —and not quite. Like Sam Rubinstein's dreadful twin who sapped his embryo companion, she, too, carried an envelope of earlier shapes: of the me as I would never again be and of my friends and mentors—puzzling, kindly, brutal, narcissistic, stimulating, and destructive people who were washed away in the second amniotic flood. Not altogether washed away, as the girl was not altogether lost. Like an old string of beads slipped from their broken thread, like a loose pile of fading snapshots, they rattle around with the golden Borsalino hat and the volume of Heine verse in a box rarely opened but palpably there; not transferable, not inheritable, immutably mine as testaments of once-upon-a-time me.